TAKE A
SEAT

16 BEAUTIFUL
PROJECTS FOR
YOUR HOME

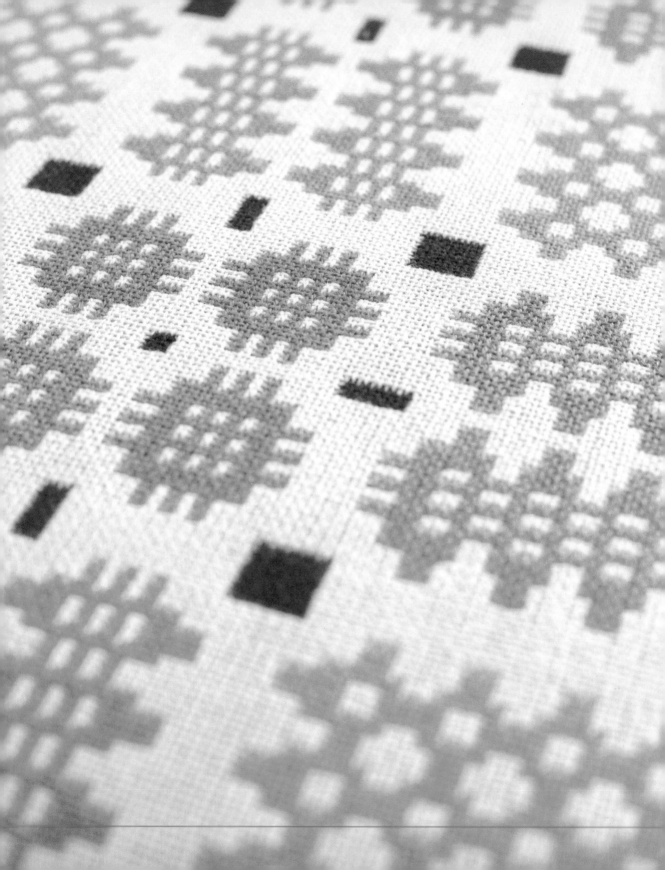

TAKE A
SEAT

16 BEAUTIFUL PROJECTS FOR YOUR HOME

Jemima Schlee

First published 2016 by
Guild of Master Craftsman Publications Ltd
Castle Place, 166 High Street, Lewes,
East Sussex BN7 1XU

Text © Jemima Schlee, 2016
Copyright in the Work © GMC Publications Ltd, 2016

ISBN 978 1 78494 111 6

While every effort has been made to obtain permission
from the copyright holders for all material used in this
book, the publishers will be pleased to hear from anyone
who has not been appropriately acknowledged and
to make the correction in future reprints.

The publishers and author can accept no legal
responsibility for any consequences arising from
the application of information, advice or instructions
given in this publication. A catalogue record for this
book is available from the British Library.

Publisher Jonathan Bailey
Production Manager Jim Bulley
Senior Project Editor Virginia Brehaut
Editor Nicola Hodgson
Managing Art Editor Gilda Pacitti
Art Editor Luana Gobbo
Step Photography Jemima Schlee and
Martha Bamford
Photographer Emma Sekhon

Colour origination by GMC Reprographics
Printed and bound in China

For Harrison and Martha

Contents

Woven-belt Chair p.46

Piped Cushion Pads p.68

Coffee-table
Footstool p.76

Giant Crochet Pouffe p.58

Garden-chair Covers p.106

Sashiko Director's Chair p.110

INTRODUCTION

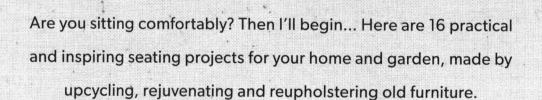

Are you sitting comfortably? Then I'll begin... Here are 16 practical and inspiring seating projects for your home and garden, made by upcycling, rejuvenating and reupholstering old furniture.

WHETHER curled up in an armchair, lounging in a garden chair or sat on a stool at a kitchen table, we all love a comfy seat. By reusing chairs, stools and benches and upcycling scrap items you can breathe new life into tired pieces and make useful, beautiful and individual furniture for your home and garden.

The projects in this book use different techniques, materials and fabrics to create unique projects that are both practical and personal. Sew simple slipcovers for garden chairs; crochet a pouffe from soft magician's rope; upholster a coffee table; or refresh stool tops with vintage-look wallpapers.

Chairs and stools can be bought fairly cheaply from junk stores, charity shops, car boot sales and auctions. However, take stock before you buy: you probably have a few pieces at home that could be given a new lease of life. The projects here vary from quick transformations such as giving kitchen chairs a fresh lick of paint, to more complex projects such as reseating a chair using leather belts and upholstering a drop-in chair seat.

Happy memories are made perched on a stool at a table full of friends, or peacefully curled up in an old armchair with a favourite book.

Spoon Seat Pads
page 40

Woven-belt Chair
page 46

Giant Crochet Pouffe
page 58

Piped Cushion Pads
page 68

Graphic Striped
Cushions **page 62**

Opposite: Coffee-table
Footstool **page 76**
This page: Crochet Stool
Toppers **page 82**

Papered Stools
page 88

Wine-crate
Stool **page 92**

Opposite: Box Cushions **page 100**
This page: Garden-chair Covers **page 106**

Opposite: Sashiko Director's Chair
page 110
This page: Crochet Bench Cushion
page 116

DINING

A lick of paint and some new fabric can completely transform a chair. You may get away with just changing the fabric cover, but if the spring of the seat has sunk slightly, it is worth refurbishing the whole item.

DROP-IN CHAIR SEAT

Supplies:

(for a seat measuring 14½in/37cm square at its widest)

- ☐ Drop-in seat chair
- ☐ Nail puller (if needed)
- ☐ Herringbone webbing tape
- ☐ ⅜in and ⅝in (10mm and 15mm) upholsterer's tacks or staples
- ☐ Upholsterer's hammer
- ☐ Web stretcher
- ☐ 24in (60cm) squares in hessian, calico, wadding and decorative top fabric
- ☐ Pencil or pen to draw template

- ☐ Sharp scissors
- ☐ Iron
- ☐ 14½ x 14½ x 2in (37 x 37 x 5cm) foam pad (length and width of the seat x 2in/5cm depth)
- ☐ Junior hacksaw, craft knife or sharp bread knife
- ☐ Staple gun
- ☐ Glass paper, white or methylated spirit, paint, paintbrush, wax or varnish (optional, if the chair needs painting)

Step 1

First, strip down the drop-in seat to its basics. If you simply need to add new fabric to the seat, remove the old fabric and go to Step 14. You may only need to take a layer or two off the existing seat. If you work right down to the basic frame, you may find old tacks left behind from previous makeovers. Remove as many as you can, as trying to hammer in a new tack and hitting an old one is very frustrating. When you are finished, you should end up with a simple, clean wooden frame.

Step 2

Now add a woven base of herringbone webbing tape. Decide how many webbing strips to use for the size of your chair: I used four, two vertical and two horizontal. Lay one end of the tape one-third along the top face of the seat frame. Align the raw cut end with the outside edge of the frame and secure it firmly with three small tacks.

Step 3

Fold the hanging end of the tape over the three tack heads and hold it down with a further two tacks (imagine the first three tacks forming the top of a letter 'w' and position these bottom two to form the lower two points of the 'w').

Step 4

Use a web stretcher to pull the webbing tape taut across the frame and achieve a drum-tight stretch. Thread a loop of the tape through the paddle slot and secure it with the wooden peg. Note which way up the paddle is: the tape will cushion the frame from any bruises and dents when you use the stretcher.

Step 5

Position the notch at the end of the paddle along the frame edge, on the opposite side to the tacked tape. Lever it up and down, pulling the tape back and forth through the slot until there is a bit of tension. You may need to play around for a while to get the feel for it.

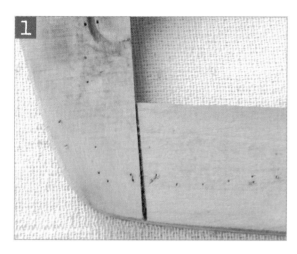

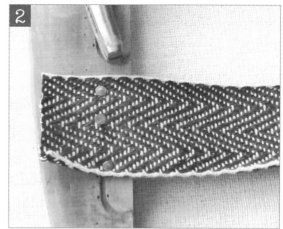

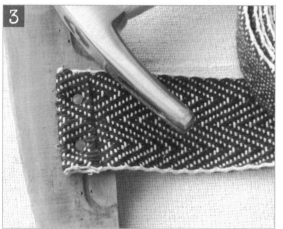

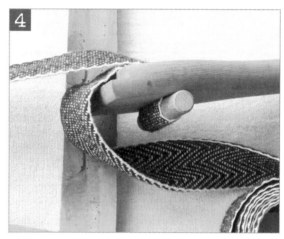

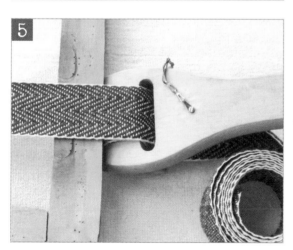

See also:
Using web stretchers *page 130*
Using an upholstery hammer *page 130*
Using glass paper *page 128*
Hand painting *page 132*

Step 6

Keep the magnetized upholsterer's hammer and some tacks to hand. Prepare the hammer with a tack on the forked magnet end. Lever the web stretcher to pull the webbing taut across the frame with your left hand if right-handed, or vice versa. Take the hammer in your other hand and give the tack a firm tap down in the centre of the tape. Swivel the hammer's head around and give the tack a few sharp hits with the other (unmagnetized) end so it is firmly hammered in. Add two more tacks, one either side of the first, as in Step 2. Trim the tape, fold it over and add the final two tacks as in Step 3. Add the other strips of webbing tape, weaving them in and out of each other.

Step 7

Now cover the webbing with a layer of hessian. Cut a piece exactly the size of the frame, using the frame itself as a template.

Step 8

Turn under all the raw edges of the hessian ⅝in (15mm) and press with an iron.

Step 9

Lay the hessian on top of the webbing with the raw edges facing downwards. Using either ⅜in (10mm) tacks or staples, secure the hessian all the way around close to the edge. If you are using staples with a hardwood frame, you may need to give them a tap or two with a hammer to set them firmly into the wood.

Step 10

Lay the calico down on your work surface. The next layer is the foam. Simply cut it to the size of the frame (use a junior hacksaw, craft knife or sharp bread knife) and centre it on top of the calico. Lay the frame, hessian side down, on top.

ORDER OF LAYERS

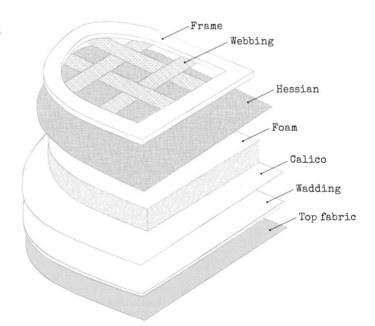

Frame
Webbing
Hessian
Foam
Calico
Wadding
Top fabric

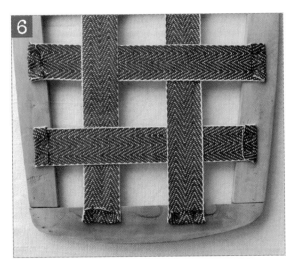

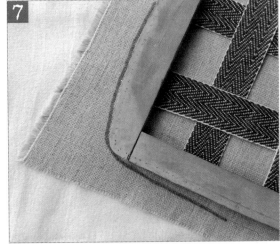

TIP

A FRIENDLY FOAM SHOP MIGHT CUT YOUR SHAPE FOR YOU IF YOU TAKE IN A TEMPLATE OF YOUR DROP-IN SEAT FRAME.

Step 11

Starting at the centre of the top furthest from you, pull the calico over the edge of the seat to the bottom surface of the frame, and secure it with a tack or staple. Do the same directly opposite at the centre of the bottom edge nearest you. Now turn the seat 90° and repeat this process with the sides of the seat.

Work methodically, tacking or stapling from the centre of each side towards the edges, turning the seat as you work. Keep the tension even and minimize any tucks and wrinkles. When you reach the corners, make neat pleats and keep the bulk of the fabric to a minimum. Trim off the excess fabric.

Step 12

Lay the wadding over the calico and smooth it across the surface with the palm of your hand. Use a staple gun to attach the wadding to the sides of the seat frame all the way around, about 3/16in (5mm) from the edge. Smooth the wadding out continually as you go to avoid forming wrinkles.

Step 13

Cut the excess wadding flush to the bottom edge of the seat frame.

Step 14

Cut the top fabric to the size of the seat frame plus 2in (5cm) all the way around and lay it right side down on your work surface. Turn the raw edges under by about 3/8in (1cm) as you stretch and fix it in position with the tacks or staples, as you did with the calico in Step 11.

Step 15

Make symmetrical pleats when you reach the corners in order to keep the fabric from puckering.

Step 16

Finally, if the chair frame itself needs an extra lift, give it a coat of paint, picking out a colour from the fabric. Dining chairs get quite a lot of wear and tear, so don't cut corners here: rub down the frame with glass paper and remove any grease from the surface before painting with white or methylated spirit. Seal the paint with wax or varnish if you don't use an acrylic or oil-based paint and allow to dry. The last step is to drop the freshly covered seat back in place.

TIP

LOOSER-WEAVE FABRIC, SUCH AS HEAVY LINEN, IS GREAT FOR THIS PROJECT AND HELPS YOU TO CREATE NICE SMOOTH CORNERS.

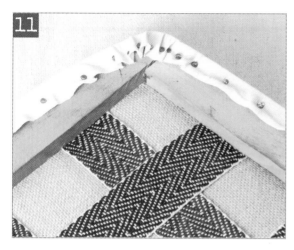

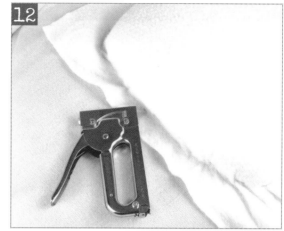

This very simple way to update an old wooden kitchen chair is also great for using up ends of paint tins or small tester pots. Paint a group of odd chairs in matching colours and turn them into a cohesive set.

PAINTED CHAIRS

Supplies:

- ☐ Spindle-back chair
- ☐ Medium and fine glass paper
- ☐ Cotton rags
- ☐ White or methylated spirit
- ☐ Leftover paint or tester pots
- ☐ 1in (2.5cm) paintbrush
- ☐ Masking fluid
- ☐ Soft wax or matt varnish

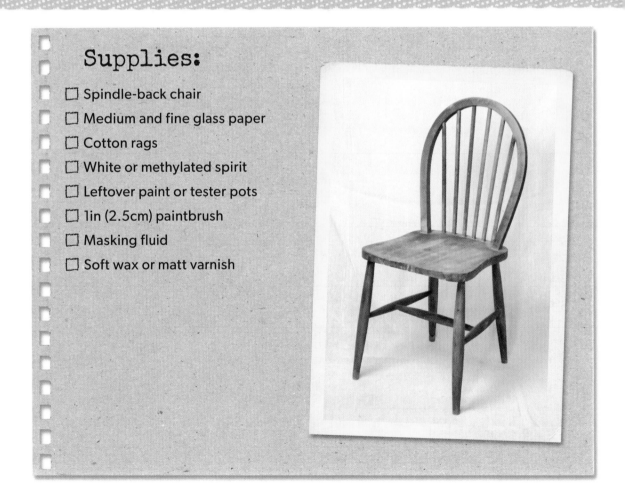

Step 1

Start by sanding down all the surfaces of the chair to remove any varnish or wax residue and give a 'key' to the wood's surface prior to painting. The most important areas from which to remove any varnish or wax are the seat and the curved frame of the chair back. Sand with medium and then fine glass paper. If your chair has a coat of varnish on it, the process will take longer. If the varnish is very thick you may need paint stripper. If you resort to this, work in a well-ventilated space and follow the manufacturer's instructions carefully.

Step 2

Wipe down every part of the chair with white or methylated spirit to get rid of any grease and dust.

Step 3

Choose which colours to apply and where, according to your personal taste. Once the wood is thoroughly dry and dust-free, you can start painting. Use a small brush to 'cut in' (see tip, above) at the edge of each colour's area. You can use masking fluid to the same end, but make sure you let the fluid dry thoroughly, following the manufacturer's instructions, before you start applying paint.

TIP

'CUTTING IN' IS USUALLY DONE WITH A SMALL BRUSH WHEN PAINTING AND ENSURES A NEAT EDGE. USING JUST A SMALL AMOUNT OF PAINT AT A TIME, MAKE SHORT STROKES TO CREATE A NEAT, SHARP LINE WHERE TWO COLOURS MEET OR A SINGLE COLOUR FINISHES. THIS IS MORE EASILY DONE WITH A FLAT-HEADED BRUSH.

Step 4

Complete the painting of each colour on the spindles, legs and struts and set the chair aside to dry completely.

Step 5

Give each colour a second coat of paint. Leave to dry completely again before adding a final coat of matt varnish or wax to every surface of the chair. Leave to dry thoroughly, following the manufacturer's instructions. If you use wax, once it is completely dry use a soft cotton cloth to buff and polish the surface.

See also:
Using glass paper *page 128*
Hand painting *page 132*

TIP

I ALWAYS LEAVE THE AREAS MOST
PRONE TO WEAR UNPAINTED. WAXING
THE BARE WOOD (STEP 5) PREVENTS
STAINING AND CREATES A WIPE-
CLEAN SURFACE.

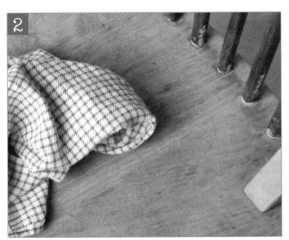

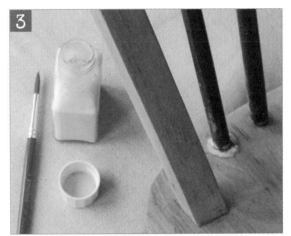

These seat pads for dining chairs are attached using small wooden spoons as toggles, which are easy to remove for laundering. You could also use metal spoons, dowelling, wooden toggles or pieces of driftwood.

SPOON SEAT PADS

Supplies:
(for a chair seat measuring 14¾ x 17in/37.5 x 43cm at its widest)

- ☐ Spindle-backed chair
- ☐ Pen and paper to make templates
- ☐ Sharp scissors
- ☐ 15 x 18 x 2in (40 x 45 x 5cm) foam pad (see Step 1 for quantity if using a different size chair)
- ☐ Permanent marker
- ☐ Junior hacksaw, craft knife or sharp bread knife
- ☐ 20in (50cm) of each fabric for outer and calico for inner (see Steps 3 and 7 for quantities)
- ☐ Iron
- ☐ Measuring tape
- ☐ Sewing thread, needle and pins
- ☐ Sewing machine and zipper foot
- ☐ 14in (36cm) zipper
- ☐ Seam ripper
- ☐ 2 x small wooden spoons (approx. 6in/15cm long)

Step 1

Make the following templates for the chair seat pad using paper and pen.

Template **A**: chair seat template. Roughly sketch the shape of the chair seat; it should reach the front and side edges, while butting up to the back or the spindles. Once you are happy with the shape, cut it out and fold it in half. Trim off any excess and make sure it is symmetrical.

Template **B**: circumference of template **A** minus 14½in (37cm) x 2¾in (7cm)

Template **C**: 16¹⁄₁₆ x 1¾in (41 x 4.5cm)

Template **D**: 3⅛ x 4in (8 x 10cm)

Step 2

Use template **A** to cut out the foam. Draw around it with a permanent marker and use a junior hacksaw, craft knife or sharp bread knife to cut the foam to shape.

Step 3

Cut two pieces of calico using template **A,** adding ⅜in (1cm) all around for the seam allowance. Fold these two pieces in half and press with an iron. Use a measuring tape to measure the circumference of the foam. Cut a strip of calico to this length, plus ¾in (2cm) x 2¾in (7cm) wide. This strip can be made up out of several strips to save on fabric – just add ¾in (2cm) seam allowance to each separate length for the joining seams. Join the strips together with ⅜in (1cm) seams and press them open. When the strip is pieced together, join the two ends with a ⅜in (1cm) seam and press open. With the pressed seams facing you, pin one long edge around one

of the pieces cut from your template. Align the raw edges as you go and use plenty of pins as you work. You are joining a curved piece of fabric to a straight piece so you need to avoid any wrinkles and tucks.

Step 4

Machine stitch a ⅜in (1cm) seam all the way around. With your work still inside out, pin the other piece cut from the template to the other long side of the strip that forms the side of the seat pad lining. Make sure the top and bottom pieces are in the same position and that their shapes mirror each other – use the pressed creases from step 3 to achieve this. Again, sew a ⅜in (1cm) seam, but this time leave a turning gap of about 12in (30cm) along the front or back edge. Reverse stitch either side of this to strengthen it. Turn right side out and insert the foam pad. This may need folding to get in, and a little teasing and tweaking to fit it snugly in position.

Step 5

Fold in the raw edges around the turning gap by ⅜in (1cm) and pin it closed.

Step 6

Hand stitch the turning gap closed using overstitch.

Step 7

Cut two pieces of outer fabric using template **A**, adding ⅜in (1cm) all around for the seam allowance. Fold these two pieces in half and press with an iron to create a crease from the centre back to the centre front of each piece. Cut one piece of outer fabric using template **B**. Cut two pieces of outer fabric from template **C**. Take the two shorter **C** strips to make the back zipper panel and place them right sides together. Align the edges and pin or tack along one long edge. Machine stitch a ⅜in (1cm)

CUTTING AND ASSEMBLY GUIDE

For each pad cut: 2 x **A**, 1 x **B**, 2 x **C** and 2 x **D**

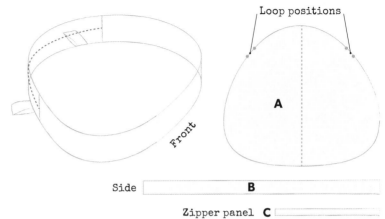

Loop positions

Front

A

Side [**B**]

Zipper panel **C** [ ]

Add ³/₈in (1cm) seam allowance around your measured pieces when cutting fabric.

Loop **D**

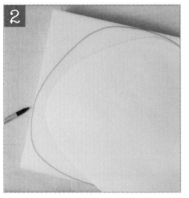

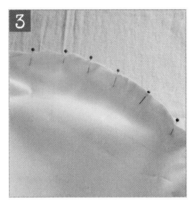

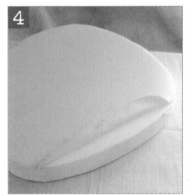

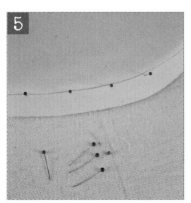

seam 1⅜in (3.5cm) long at either end, reverse stitching at each end for strength. Reset the machine to its longest stitch and sew a temporary ⅜in (1cm) seam between the two short end seams.

Step 8

Press this seam open and lay the zipper face down along the temporary stitching. Pin or tack in place.

Step 9

Turn to the right side and use a zipper foot to sew in the zipper. Undo the temporary seam.

Step 10

Lay the longer strip of fabric face up in front of you. Place the zipper panel of fabric face down on top of the right-hand side of it and align the right-hand edges. Pin or tack and stitch a ⅜in (1cm) seam.

Step 11

Press the seam away from the zipper panel. Do the same with the remaining two short raw ends to complete the side panel.

Step 12

Make two loops: cut two pieces of outer fabric using template **D**. Fold one in half right sides together so it is 3⅛ x 4in (8 x 10cm). Align, pin or tack the long edges and sew a ³⁄₈in (1cm) seam along it. Turn right

See also:

Inserting a zipper *page 142*
Topstitch *page 137*
Overstitch *page 146*
Covering foam pads *page 133*

side out and press. Topstitch along the two long edges. Make a second loop in the same way.

Step 13

Place the cushion template on the chair and use it to find the position and length you need to make the loops for the spoons. The position will be central between two spindles on either side. The length can be judged by slotting a spoon through the folded loop, then pulling it snugly against the spindles. Measure a point ³⁄₈in (1cm) beyond the edge of the template. Trim the (still folded) loop to length.

Step 14

Having cut the loops to size, pin or tack them, folded, into position onto one piece **A** of outer fabric, on the right side and with the raw edges aligned, the folded end pointing towards the centre of the fabric.

Step 15

Find the centre of the zipper panel and align it with the centre back of piece **A** with the loops. As in Step 3, carefully join the side piece to the piece all the way around, using either pins or tacking.

Step 16

Sew a ³⁄₈in (1cm) seam all the way around. Open the zipper slightly before pinning or tacking the second piece **A** to the remaining raw edge of the side panel.

Step 17

Stitch a ³⁄₈in (1cm) seam around this edge.

Step 18

Press all the seams to one side. Turn right way out through the opening and insert the cushion pad.

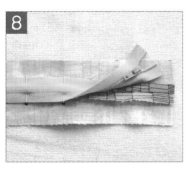

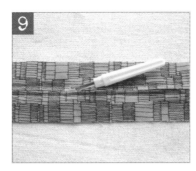

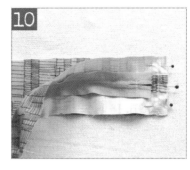

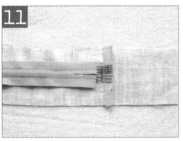

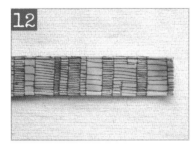

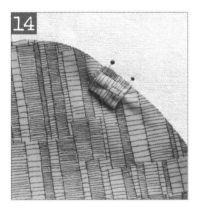

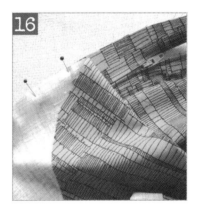

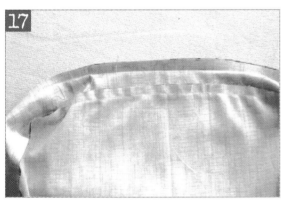

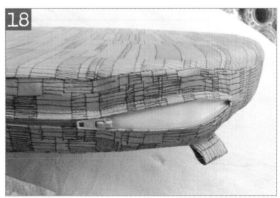

Leather belts can be picked up very cheaply and, when woven together, make a sturdy and hardwearing seat. Use belts in various widths and colours, monochrome or textured, to create different patterns.

WOVEN-BELT CHAIR

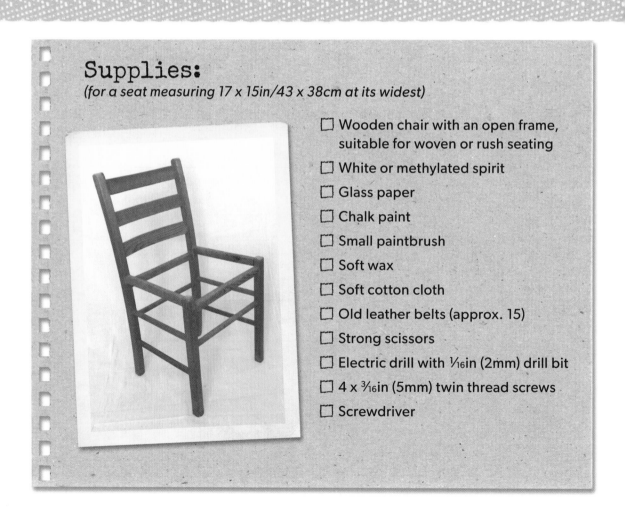

Supplies:
(for a seat measuring 17 x 15in/43 x 38cm at its widest)

- [ ] Wooden chair with an open frame, suitable for woven or rush seating
- [ ] White or methylated spirit
- [ ] Glass paper
- [ ] Chalk paint
- [ ] Small paintbrush
- [ ] Soft wax
- [ ] Soft cotton cloth
- [ ] Old leather belts (approx. 15)
- [ ] Strong scissors
- [ ] Electric drill with $\frac{1}{16}$in (2mm) drill bit
- [ ] 4 x $\frac{3}{16}$in (5mm) twin thread screws
- [ ] Screwdriver

Step 1

Strip any rush or woven seating from the chair if it has any. If the wood is untreated, simply wipe it all over with white spirit or methylated spirit to remove any grease or dust. If the surface is polished or waxed, rub it down with glass paper first. Now give the chair frame a good coat of paint. I used chalk paint as it gives a solid, flat surface. One coat should be enough. Follow it by a coat of soft wax once the paint is fully dry.

Step 2

Lay out the leather belts and remove the buckles, either by cutting them off or by removing the stitching or studs by which they are attached.

Step 3

Decide which belts to use and in which order, and whether to use plain or coloured, smooth or textured. Work out your pattern by weaving the belts in and out of each other. Experiment until you are happy with the pattern.

Step 4

All the screw fixings will be made on the under edge of the seat frame's four sides. Take the belt that runs centrally and from front to back of the practice pattern, as arranged in the previous step. When the belt is in position, the end of it lined up with the inside edge of the frame, drill pilot holes through both the leather and the wood to facilitate fixing in small screws with a screwdriver.

TIP

IF YOU CAN FIND LONG BELTS, YOU MAY BE ABLE TO GET TWO LENGTHS FROM EACH, NEEDING FEWER OVERALL.

Step 5

With the chair still upside down, wrap the leather belt over the seat frame to the front edge. Make sure the drill, screws and screwdriver are within easy reach. Pull the belt taut; while doing so, drill further pilot holes through the leather and the wood before fixing more screws.

Step 6

Cut off the excess belt leather flush along the inside edge of the chair frame.

Step 7

Add the next leather belt following Steps 4–6, this time from one side to the other of the seat frame. Continue attaching belts alternately from front to back and side to side, working out towards the corners of the seat frame. Weave the belts in and out of each other as you do so.

Step 8

As you reach the corners, the whole woven seat will become more taut. The outer few belts will need to be fed in and out of the fixed ones methodically before being pulled taut and screwed down.

Step 9

When the seat frame is completely filled, tighten all the screws firmly and trim any crooked leather ends.

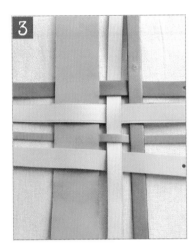

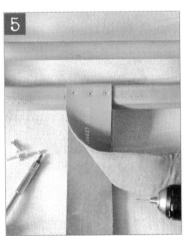

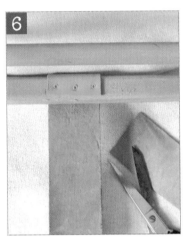

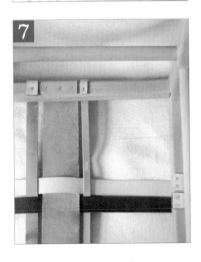

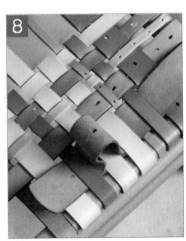

LIVING

Use an old blanket to make a new cover for a much-loved armchair – perfect use for a favourite wool blanket that has seen better days. Felted wool creates a hardwearing fabric for a chair seat.

BLANKET SEAT PAD

Supplies:
(for a seat pad measuring 20 x 20 x 4in/51 x 51 x 10cm at its widest)

- [ ] Armchair with loose seat pad
- [ ] Paper, pencil and measuring tape to make templates
- [ ] Sharp scissors
- [ ] Old blanket or thick woollen fabric (see step 1 for quantities)
- [ ] Sewing thread, needle and pins
- [ ] Sewing machine and zipper foot
- [ ] Iron
- [ ] 2 x zippers (mine were 22in/55cm long)
- [ ] Seam ripper
- [ ] Linen or wool yarn for blanket-stitch edging
- [ ] Yarn needle

Step 1

Make a template for the cover. You could simply draw around the seat pad if it is firm enough. However, if it is soft or has become distorted through wear or age, it may be better to take the measurements from the seat of the chair.

Template **A**: top and bottom of the seat pad plus ⅜in (1cm) all around for seam allowance.

Template **B**: front edge of the seat pad plus 9in (23cm) in length and ¾in (2cm) in width.

Template **C**: the two sides and back edges of the seat pad, minus 6¾in (17cm) in length, by half the width plus ¾in (2cm).

Cut two pieces of fabric with template **A**, one piece with template **B**, and two pieces with template **C** (see diagram opposite).

Step 2

Prepare the zipper panel. Take the two pieces of fabric cut from template **C** and place them right sides together. Pin or tack the two together along one long edge. Machine stitch a ⅜in (1cm) seam at either end, 2in (5cm) long, reverse stitching at either end for strength. Change the machine stitch to the longest setting and stitch a ⅜in (1cm) seam in the gap between the two 2in (5cm) seams – do not reverse stitch at the ends this time, as this is just a temporary seam.

Step 3

Press open the seam from Step 2 with a warm iron.

Step 4

With the wrong side of the work facing you, find the centre point along the seam. Place the two zippers right side down along the pressed seam, the tag/opening ends butting up to one another at the centre point. Their ends should finish just beyond the start of the short seam at either end. Pin or tack the zippers in place. Turn the work over and, using the zipper foot on your sewing machine, stitch the zippers in ³⁄₁₆in (5mm) from the central seam.

Step 5

Stitch back and forth across the ends several times for extra strength.

Step 6

With the zipper piece facing right side up, place fabric piece **B** right side down on top of it, aligning the two short left-hand ends. Pin or tack this short end before stitching a ⅝in (1.5cm) seam along it, reverse stitching at either end for strength.

Step 7

Press this seam away from the zipper. Turn the work over so that it is right side up, then topstitch ⅜in (1cm) from the seam along the **B** side of the seam. Repeat this seam construction at the other end of both the zipper piece and piece **B** to create a circular fabric strip.

See also:

Inserting a zipper *page 142*
Topstitch *page 137*
Blanket stitch *page 146*

CUTTING AND ASSEMBLY GUIDE

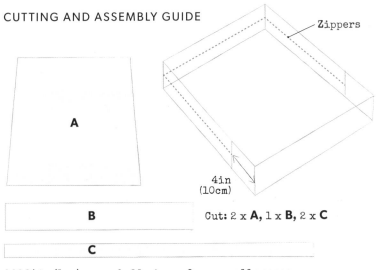

Zippers

A

4in
(10cm)

B

C

Cut: 2 x **A**, 1 x **B**, 2 x **C**

Add ³⁄₈in (1cm) around all pieces for seam allowance

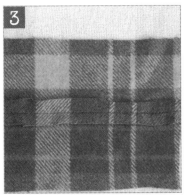

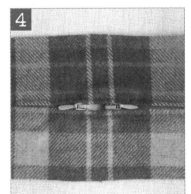

Step 8

Lay one piece of fabric **A** right side up in front of you. Lay the circular fabric strip face down on top of it, aligning the centre where the zippers meet with the centre back of piece **A**. Pin or tack both pieces together along this edge.

Step 9

Starting ⅜in (1cm) from one end of the pinned or tacked back edge, stitch a ⅜in (1cm) seam, stopping ⅜in (1cm) from the other end. Reverse stitch at the beginning and end of this seam for extra strength.

Step 10

To turn the corner, manipulate the fabric, pivoting at the point where the seam stitching ended, turning it 90°, and aligning the continuing edge of the circular fabric strip with the side of piece **A**. Pin or tack carefully, then repeat Step 9 along this edge, too.

Step 11

Do the same with the remaining two edges. You may need to tweak and stretch the material a little if the fabric edges are not exactly the same length, but hopefully this will not be the case. Use a seam ripper to open up the temporary seam over the zippers made in Step 2.

Step 12

Open both zippers by about 4in (10cm) before repeating the process from Step 8 to attach the second piece **A**.

Step 13

Carefully press the seams away from the circular fabric strip and towards the **A** pieces before turning the seat cover out through the zipper gap.

Step 14

Use a pencil or crochet hook to prod the corners out from inside to make them neat and sharp. There is no need to trim or snip them before turning right way out as the bulk of fabric will help fill the corners where the pad may not reach.

Step 15

Using linen or wool yarn doubled, thread a yarn needle and embellish the edge of the seat top and bottom with blanket stitch (see page 146). Make each stitch about ½in (12mm) long. As you sew, you will be encasing the seam selvedge within the stitch and therefore reducing the fraying of the raw fabric edges on the inside.

Step 16

Make three stitches at each corner in order to turn to the next edge neatly.

Step 17

Finally, open the zippers fully and insert the seat pad.

TIP

IF YOU ARE USING A BLANKET, YOU MAY WANT TO FELT IT BEFOREHAND, ALTHOUGH THIS ONLY WORKS WITH 100% WOOL FABRIC. WASH AT A HIGH TEMPERATURE WITHOUT USING SOFTENER, ADDING AN OLD TOWEL FOR FRICTION – THIS WILL HELP THE FELTING PROCESS DURING THE WASHING AND SPINNING CYCLES.

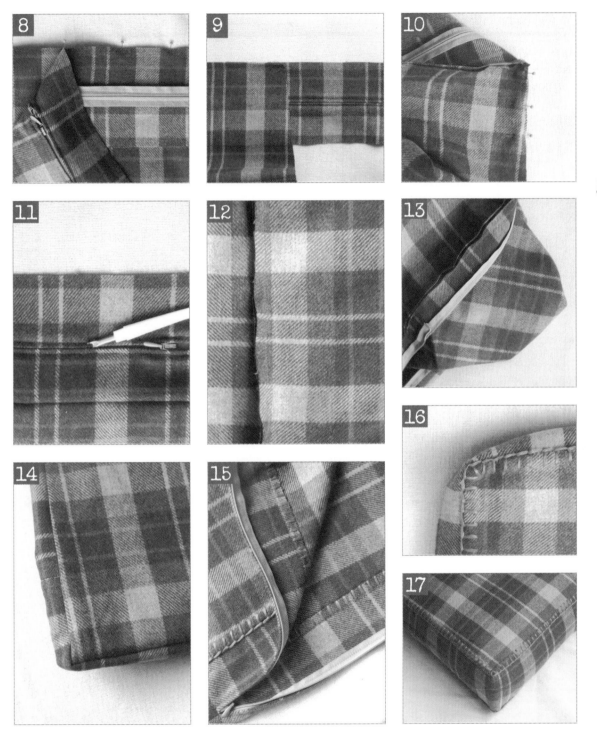

More rigid than the crochet surface might suggest, this pouffe makes a great footstool, seat or coffee table. Close to a Moroccan leather pouffe in density, its size and stability make this a very versatile item.

GIANT CROCHET POUFFE

Supplies:
(to make a pouffe 24in/60cm diameter x 12in/30cm high)

- ☐ 220yd (200m) cotton magician's rope ⅜in (1cm) in diameter in sage green (A)
- ☐ 220yd (200m) cotton magician's rope ⅜in (1cm) in diameter in olive (B)
- ☐ 8mm (UK0:USL/11) crochet hook (or a larger one if you like)
- ☐ Sharp scissors
- ☐ Stuffing (I used two duvets)

TIP

THIS POUFFE COULD BE MADE USING STRIPS OF OLD FABRIC. TORN EDGES WOULD GIVE THE PIECE A LOVELY, SOFT, WORN-LOOKING FINISH, A GREAT WAY OF USING UP OLD BEDLINEN.

Step 1

This pouffe is made in two halves then joined together when stuffed. Work in one direction only, not turning the work between rows. Start with A by making a slip knot, then ch 5 and join with a sl st. (See page 147 for Crochet Techniques.)

Step 2

Ch 2, *tr 1, ch 1; repeat from * until you have worked 10 tr into the ring. Join to first ch 2 with a sl st (20 sts).

Step 3

Ch 1, work 1 round of dc, working into the top of every stitch from the previous round. Join to first ch 1 with a sl st (20 sts).

Step 4

Ch 2, tr 1 into the base of the ch 2, tr 2 into the top of the next st and all the remaining sts from the previous round. Join to first ch 2 with a sl st (40 sts).

Step 5

Ch 1, work 1 row in dc, working into the top of every stitch from the previous row. Join to first ch 1 with a sl st (40 sts).

Step 6

Ch 1, *tr 1 into next st, tr 2 into the following st; repeat from * until you have worked a complete round (60 sts).

Step 7

Next four rounds: ch 1, work 1 row in dc, working into the top of every stitch from the previous row. Join to first ch 1 with a sl st (60 sts). The first half of the pouffe is now complete. Cut the tail end of A to 12in (30cm). Use the hook to pull it through the final loop to finish. Put this piece to one side.

Step 8

Repeat Steps 1–7 with colour B for the second half of the pouffe, but leave a tail of rope 6½yd (6m) when you finish. Fill any gaps through which the stuffing might show by using the hook to weave a length of rope through the back of the central treble stitches.

Step 9

Place the two halves wrong sides together and start to join them. Starting with tail end A, push the hook through the top of a stitch along the edge of half B, from the front to the back. Wrap the rope around the hook and draw the whole tail of the rope through. Now insert the hook through the stitch above in half A, from the back to the front, wrap with rope A, and pull through to the back of the work. Now insert the hook from back to front in the next stitch in half A. Wrap tail end B around the hook and pull the whole tail through to the back. Insert the hook from front to back of the next stitch on half B, wrap rope B and pull it through to the front of the work. This forms the first two stitches. You are, in effect, joining the two halves with overstitch (see page 146), using alternative colours.

Step 10

Continue until you have completed three-quarters of the circumference. Stuff the pouffe through the gap in the join, filling it as firmly as possible.

Step 11

Close the stuffing gap with overstitching. You can do it quite loosely, pulling and tweaking the rope stitches with your fingers at the end. To finish off, hook both of the ends through to the front between the two halves. Tie a tight knot, trim the tail ends to about 6in (15cm), and push them back through to the inside of the work.

TIP

YOU MAY NEED TO
TWEAK THE JOINING
STITCHES UNTIL
THEY LOOK EVEN.

Refresh your sofa with these patched cushions from a simple striped fabric reassembled into geometric designs. You could use anything from deckchair stripes to simple mattress ticking to create the same effect.

62 GRAPHIC STRIPED CUSHIONS

Supplies:
(to make a 17¾in/45cm square cushion)

- [ ] 21½ x 43in (55 x 110cm) of striped fabric for each cushion
- [ ] Measuring tape
- [ ] Sharp scissors
- [ ] Iron
- [ ] Sewing thread, needle and pins
- [ ] Sewing machine and zipper foot
- [ ] 16in (40cm) zipper
- [ ] Seam ripper
- [ ] 17¾in (45cm) square cushion pad
- [ ] Knitting needle or crochet hook

Step 1

Cut the rectangle of fabric in half to make two pieces 21½in (55cm) square – you want two squares where the stripes are identically positioned. If the stripes are fairly wide you may need more fabric to achieve identical positions. Place the two squares of fabric on top of one another, right sides together, aligning the stripes.

Step 2

Fold the top right-hand corner of the top layer of fabric down to meet the bottom left-hand corner, creating a fold upon the diagonal. Press the diagonal fold with a hot iron. Open the top layer of fabric out flat again and make two more creases with the iron, each one ⅜in (1cm) to either side of the first diagonal fold.

Step 3

Turn the top right-hand edge down again along the upper fold. Thread a needle and sew along the fold, joining the two pieces of fabric with overstitches about ⅜in (1cm) apart. Manipulate the fabric as you go so that all the stripes meet, creating a sharp chevron. The creases you have pressed are on the bias, which means that your fabric will stretch. Ease it carefully so the stripes from the top and bottom layer fabric squares meet neatly.

Step 4

Open the top layer of fabric out flat again. Rotate your work 180° and repeat Step 3, folding the top right-hand corner down along the upper crease and overstitching along it. Open the fabric out flat again. Give the work a light press with an iron and then machine stitch along the two outer creases where you have overstitched. Remove the overstitching and cut the joined fabric on the diagonal between the two lines of stitching, leaving ⅜in (1cm) seam selvedges on each side.

Step 5

Press the diagonal seams of both squares of fabric open.

Step 6

When you turn over the work you should have good, sharp chevrons formed from the diagonal join of the stripes.

Step 7

Place the two squares of fabric right sides together, with the diagonal seams lying on top of each other, and repeat Steps 2–5.

TIP

TO TURN CORNERS WHEN USING A SEWING MACHINE, LEAVE THE NEEDLE DOWN AS YOU REACH THE POINT FOR TURNING, RAISE THE MACHINE FOOT AND THEN SWIVEL THE WORK 90° BEFORE LOWERING THE FOOT AND CONTINUING TO THE NEXT CORNER.

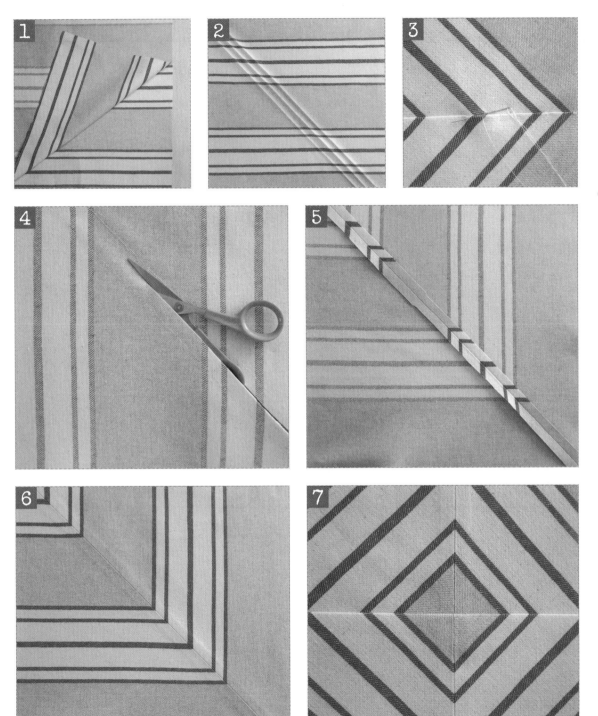

Step 8

After cutting, press these two new diagonal seams open.

Step 9

You now have the pieces for the front and back squares of the cushion cover – one with an 'X' and one with a '+'.

Step 10

Place your two squares of fabric right sides together and trim them neatly along all four edges so that they measure 18½ x 18½in (47 x 47cm). Pin or tack along one edge. Sew two ⅜in (1cm) seams from either end of this edge and 1½in (4cm) long. Reverse stitch at either end of these seams for extra strength. Now set the machine to its longest stitch and sew a temporary ⅜in (1cm) seam between the two short seams. Press open the seams along this edge with a hot iron.

Step 11

Lay the zipper right side down along the pressed temporary seam and pin it in position.

Step 12

Turn the work over so the right side is facing you and tack around the zipper before removing the pins from the other side.

Step 13

With the right side facing you, stitch around the zipper about ³⁄₁₆in (5mm) from the seam, using a zipper foot. Reverse stitch back and forth a few times across either end to give it extra strength. Remove the tacking and open up the temporary seam using a seam ripper.

Step 14

With the zipper seam furthest from you, and the zipper about 6in (15cm) open, align all the raw edges and pin or tack along them before sewing a ⅜in (1cm) seam all the way around.

Step 15

Turn the cushion cover right side out through the open zipper.

Step 16

Use a knitting needle or crochet hook to prod the four corners from the inside of the cushion cover to make them crisp and pointed, then give them a good press with a hot iron. Finally, insert the cushion pad.

See also:
Inserting a zipper *page 142*
Overstitch *page 146*

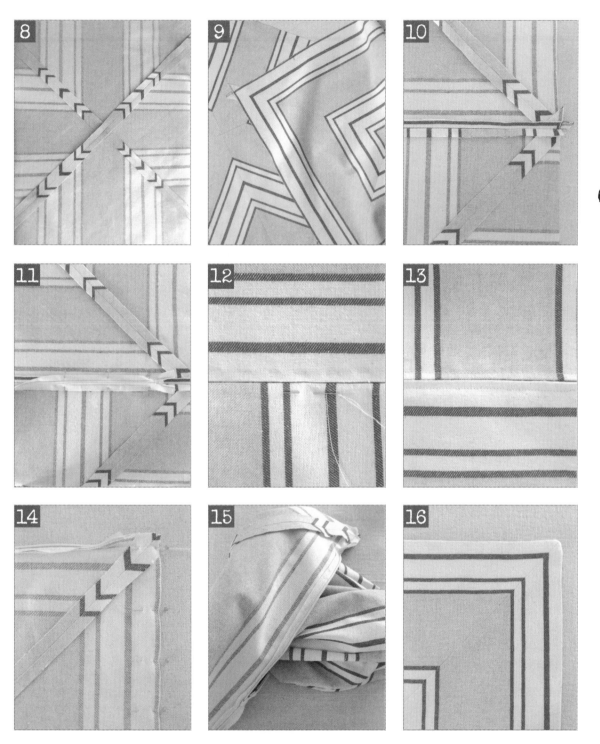

This crisp linen cover outlined with piping and decorated with fabric buttons can be made as sober or as jazzy as you like. Keep to a limited palette of colours or make merry with all your bright fabric scraps.

PIPED CUSHION PADS

Supplies:
(to fit 21⅝in/55cm square and 21⅝ x 17¾in/55 x 45cm loose seat pads)

- ☐ Armchair with loose cushion pads
- ☐ Paper, pencil and measuring tape for making templates
- ☐ Sharp scissors
- ☐ Plain linen fabric (see Step 1 for quantities)
- ☐ 9yd (8.25m) of contrasting fabric for covering piping cut on the bias (see Step 1 for quantities)
- ☐ 9yd (8.25m) of piping cord (twice the circumference of each cushion plus 6in/15cm)
- ☐ Sewing thread, needle and pins
- ☐ Sewing machine and zipper foot
- ☐ Iron
- ☐ Strong waxed linen thread or strong thread
- ☐ 16 x ¾in (2cm) diameter self-cover buttons
- ☐ Scraps of fabric for covering buttons
- ☐ Mattress needle

CUTTING AND ASSEMBLY GUIDE

For each pad cut: 2 each x **A (back)** and **A (seat)** 1 x **B**, 1 x **C**

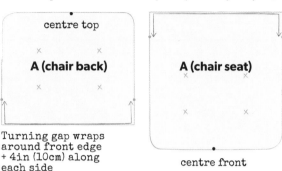

centre top

A (chair back)

A (chair seat)

Turning gap wraps
around front edge
+ 4in (10cm) along
each side

centre front

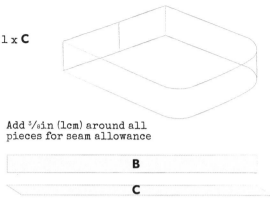

Add ³∕₈in (1cm) around all
pieces for seam allowance

B

C

Step 1

Take measurements from the armchair cushion
pads in order to make the templates to cut the
fabric. For each cushion you will need a top and
bottom piece, **A**, and a strip for the sides, **B**, that
measures the depth of the cushion plus ¾in (2cm)
x the circumference plus 4in (10cm). You also need
two bias strips, **C**, each one measuring 1½in (4cm)
x the length of piece **B**. Cut the piping cord in half
and cover each half with a strip of bias-cut fabric **C**.
Lay the piping along the centre of the wrong side of
the fabric strip and fold the fabric over to encase the
cord, aligning the two long raw edges of the fabric.
Tack if you wish. Then, using a zipper foot, machine
stitch starting 4in (10cm) from one end, as snugly as
you can against the cord, stopping 4in (10cm) from
the far end.

Step 2

Trim the raw edges of the fabric-covered bias to
exactly ³∕₈in (1cm) from the stitch line below the cord.

Step 3

Lay one fabric piece **A** right side up in front of
you. Mark a point at the centre as marked on the
template. Line up the centre of one piece of covered

piping cord with the centre front of the fabric,
aligning the raw edges of the covered cord with the
raw edges of piece **A**. Tack the piping to the fabric,
working first in one direction then the other to
complete the circumference. Gently ease the bias
piping around the curved corners.

Step 4

At the right-angled corners, snip from the raw
edge up to the line of stitching on the piping, taking
care not to cut the stitching itself. Do this ³∕₈in (1cm)
before the corner. Turn your piping 90° as tightly
and neatly as you can, and continue tacking it down
along the next edge.

Step 5

When you reach 4in (10cm) from where the two
ends of the piping meet at the centre back of piece
A, trim each end ³∕₈in (1cm) longer than it needs to
be to join snugly. Stitch a ³∕₈in (1cm) seam to join the
two ends and press the seam open. Trim the two
piping cord ends to butt up with one another. Fold
the bias fabric over and finish tacking it down.

Step 6

With the zipper foot on your machine, stitch snugly
along the tacking to join the piping to the fabric.

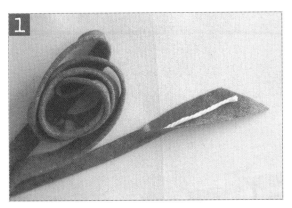

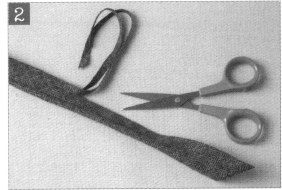

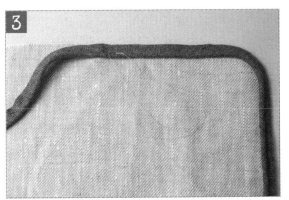

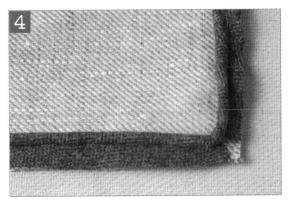

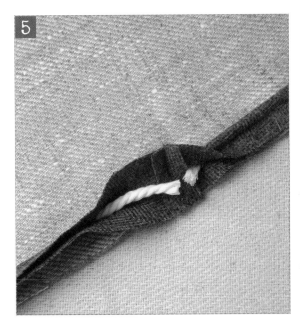

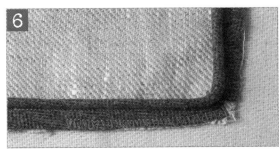

See also:

Self-covered buttons *page 144*

Trimming corners and curves *page 138*

Stain proofing *page 134*

Step 7

Take piece **B**, fold one short edge over by ⅜in (1cm) and press it. Place it down with the raw edge of the fold facing you and lining up with the final join you made in the piping. Tack piece **B** all the way around, covering the piping and with all the raw edges aligned. When you complete the circumference, trim the end ⅜in (1cm) longer than it needs to be to meet the fold you pressed earlier.

Step 8

Align the two raw short ends of piece **B** and pin or tack them together. Stitch a ⅜in (1cm) seam and press it open. Complete tacking **B** into position before using a zipper foot to stitch snugly up to the piping all the way around with a ⅜in (1cm) seam.

Step 9

Repeat Steps 3–8 with the remaining piece **A** and the second piece of covered piping, this time reading 'top' for 'front' and 'bottom' for 'back'. This time, leave a turning gap starting 4in (10cm) along one side and before the back edge, missing out the two corners and finishing 4in (10cm) along the other side beyond the back edge. Start and finish the seam with reverse stitching at the opening of the turning gap to give it extra strength. Turn right side out through the gap and ease it over the cushion pad. Fold the edge of the turning gap in on either side and pin it closed, ready for hand stitching.

Step 10

Using strong waxed linen thread (or standard strong thread doubled), hand stitch the turning gap closed, pushing the needle up through the seam joining the piping and piece **A**, making a small backstitch, and pushing the needle back down through the seam to catch the folded edge of piece **B.**

Step 11

Cover the buttons following the instructions on the packaging (see page 144).

Step 12

Arrange four buttons on one side of each cushion. Mark their positions with pins before turning over and marking corresponding positions on the other side. Use a measuring tape and be methodical to ensure they align correctly. Mine looked best 6in (15cm) in from the sides and from the front/top edges. This left a larger gap between the buttons and the back edge of the seat cushion, which is covered by the back cushion when in position.

Step 13

Use waxed linen thread and a mattress needle to attach each pair of buttons. Leave a tail of about 8in (20cm) when you push the needle through from one side of the cushion to the other.

Step 14

Feed the needle through the button. If the needle is too thick for the hole in the button, unthread it, pass the thread through the button, then rethread the needle. Push the needle back through to the other side, then feed the thread through the second button. Repeat this so that the strong thread has passed through both buttons twice, finally pushing the needle out through the side you started from.

Step 15

With both tails of thread emerging at the same side, tug them firmly to tighten them and slightly pucker the cushion between the two buttons. Tie the tail ends together while still taut. Thread each of the four thread ends individually on to the mattress needle and 'lose' them inside the cushion.

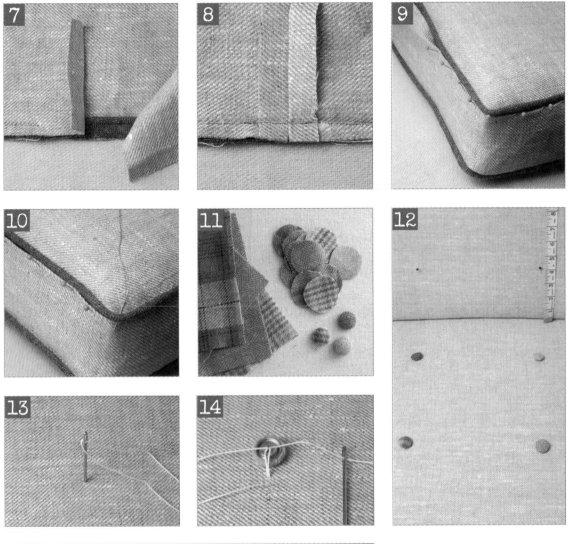

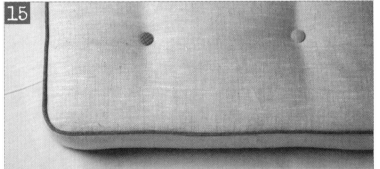

TIP

THESE COVERS ARE NOT
REMOVABLE AS THEY
ARE BUTTONED. IT IS
THEREFORE A GOOD
IDEA TO STAIN PROOF
THEM (SEE PAGE 134).

OCCASIONAL

This footstool is made from an old double school desk and has two little bookshelves just below the surface – perfect for storing newspapers and magazines. It also doubles up as extra seating at gatherings.

COFFEE-TABLE FOOTSTOOL

Supplies:
(for a tabletop 39⅜ x 16¼in/100 x 41cm)

- ☐ Wooden coffee table or simple desk
- ☐ Saw
- ☐ Fine glass paper
- ☐ Non-slip rubber matting the dimensions of the tabletop (optional)
- ☐ Sharp scissors
- ☐ 39⅜ x 16¼ x 6in (100 x 41 x 15cm) foam pad (buy this pre-cut to size: length and width of the coffee table x 6in/15cm depth)
- ☐ Measuring tape
- ☐ 60 x 36in (150 x 90cm) in each of calico and top fabric (see step 3 for quantities)
- ☐ Upholsterer's hammer and tacks
- ☐ Sewing needle, pins and strong thread, or standard thread doubled
- ☐ 116in (3m) of trimming ribbon (circumference of tabletop plus 4in/10cm)
- ☐ Fabric glue

Step 1
Mark and saw the legs off your piece so that its top stands 13½in (34cm) from the floor. Rub the sharp sawn edges with glass paper to remove any splinters and burrs if necessary.

Step 2
The foam has a tendency to slip about as you work. This can be avoided if you cut a piece of non-slip rubber matting to fit and place it on the tabletop.

Step 3
Place the foam pad on top of the non-slip rubber. Use a measuring tape to work out how much calico you will need to cover the pad with enough to tack it to the edges of the tabletop. Cut the calico with an excess of 1½in (4cm) all around – or a little more if you like, as you can trim it at the end of Step 4.

Step 4
Cover the foam pad with calico. Keep the magnetized upholsterer's hammer and some tacks to hand. Get the hammer ready with a tack on the forked magnet end. Lay the calico over the foam and, folding the raw edge under by about ⅝in (1.5cm), centre one end on the edge of the tabletop. Take the hammer in your other hand and firmly tap the tack down to nail the fabric to the wood. Swivel the hammer's head around to give the tack a few sharp hits with the other (unmagnetized) end so that it is firmly hammered in. Add a few more tacks to either side of the first, each about 1½in (4cm) apart. Do the same at the opposite end, keeping the tension of the calico across the foam as consistent as possible, turning the edge under by ⅝in (1.5cm) again and trimming off any excess.

Step 5
Repeat the process of Step 4 on the other two sides, keeping the surface of the fabric as taut and smooth as possible.

Step 6
When you have worked out towards the corners, smooth the excess calico to the folded points. Cut off any extra fabric at 45°, leaving about 1½in (4cm) of overhang on each side.

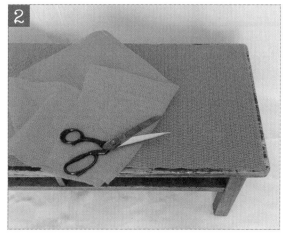

Step 7

Take time to fold and tuck the raw edges in and pin them to form a crisp, neat corner.

Step 8

Hand stitch the corner seam using overstitch and strong thread or normal thread doubled.

Step 9

Add one final tack on the corner of the footstool to keep everything secure.

Step 10

Now add the top layer of fabric. Spend some time lining up its position over the footstool until you are happy with the way the pattern on it lies. Work in the same way as Steps 4–9. There is no need to turn under the edges of the fabric as you will be covering them with the trimming ribbon and you do not want to create too much bulk.

Step 11

Glue the trimming ribbon around the bottom edge of the seat, fixing it down using fabric glue and covering the tacks and raw edges of the top layer. Hold down the beginning edge of the ribbon with a small tack.

Step 12

When you complete the circumference, trim to overlap by 1in (2.5cm), fold the raw edge under and glue to cover the raw beginning end. You can use a small tack or nail to hold this in place if you wish. Pin the trim into position all the way around while the glue dries.

TIP

I USED A BEAUTIFUL OLD WELSH BLANKET THAT HAD BEEN ATTACKED BY MOTHS, USING THE LEAST DAMAGED PART TO COVER MY FOOTSTOOL. IF YOU USE A BLANKET, YOU MAY WANT TO FELT IT BEFOREHAND, ALTHOUGH THIS ONLY WORKS WITH 100% WOOL FABRIC. WASH AT A HIGH TEMPERATURE WITHOUT USING SOFTENER, ADDING AN OLD TOWEL FOR FRICTION – THIS WILL HELP THE FELTING PROCESS DURING THE WASHING AND SPINNING CYCLES.

See also:
Overstitch page 146
Using a saw page 129
Using an upholstery hammer page 130
Using glass paper page 128

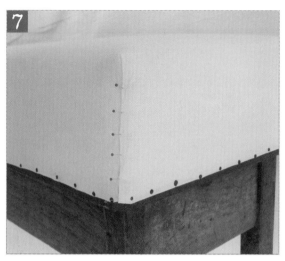

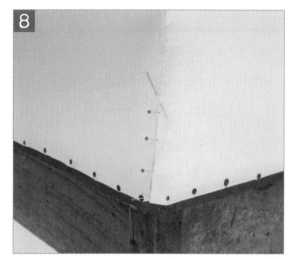

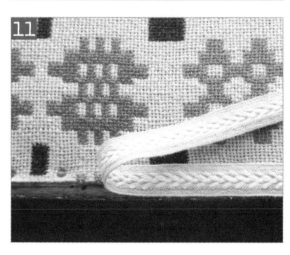

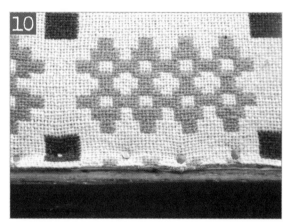

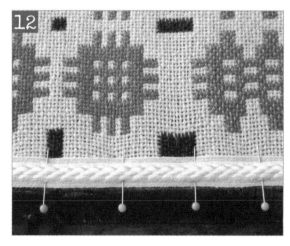

Stools are handy for large gatherings, but can be challenging to sit on during a long meal with good friends. A crocheted chunky wool topper makes them more comfortable and allows you to add a little colour to a room.

CROCHET STOOL TOPPERS

Supplies:

(for one stool top measuring 12in/30cm square; options also given for circular and oval stool tops)

- [ ] Square-topped stool (see Step 5 for an oval or circular stool)
- [ ] Glass paper, paint, paintbrush, white or methylated spirit (optional)
- [ ] Paper, pencil and measuring tape to make template
- [ ] Sharp scissors
- [ ] 2 x 100g balls of Rowan Big Wool, 100% wool (87yd/80m per 100g ball); I used 069 Reseda (light green), 054 Vert (aqua green) and 007 Smoky (dark grey)
- [ ] 5mm (UK6:USH/8) crochet hook
- [ ] 6mm (UK4:USJ/10) crochet hook
- [ ] Yarn needle
- [ ] Tailors' chalk
- [ ] Sewing machine

Step 1

Start off by drawing up a template. Turn the stool upside down and place the seat on a sheet of paper. Draw around it with a pencil. Measure the two dimensions – length and width – and mark them down along the edges. If the stool's seat is circular or ovoid (see step 6), mark down the measurements at its longest and widest points.

Step 2

See Crochet Techniques, page 147. Make a tension square as follows. Make a slip knot and chain 10 for the foundation row, ch 2, turn. Tr into 3rd ch from hook (counts as 1 tr) and into the remaining 9 sts of the foundation row, ch 2, turn. Work six rows of basketweave stitch (see box). Finish off by cutting the yarn to 4in (10cm) and drawing it through the last st. Give the tension square a quick press and measure it.

Now for a bit of maths: you will need to work out the number of stitches you need for the foundation row by counting how many stitches will make up the width of your template. Keep to multiples of 6 stitches plus 4. It is always better to have a snug fit than a baggy one, so round your total number of stitches down rather than up if you need to. Do not worry about the length at this point – you can measure the work against your template as it progresses. My measurement was 1⅜in (3.5cm) across 15 stitches; this worked out as 40 ch for the foundation row, plus 2 to turn.

Step 3

Crochet the top surface of the stool topper using the 6mm hook, working in basketweave stitch until you have made a piece of fabric the same size as your template.

BASKETWEAVE STITCH

Make the foundation chain – multiples of 6 plus 4.

Setting-up row: Tr in the 3rd chain from hook, tr in all sts of foundation chain. When you get to the end of the row, ch 2 and turn.

Row 1: Skip the first tr from previous row, * tptr into the next 3 sts, and bptr into the following 3 sts, repeat from * to end, tr in top ch of turning ch from the row below, ch 2, turn.

Rows 2 and 3: Repeat row 1.

Row 4: Skip the first tr, * bptr into the next 3 sts from the previous row, and fptr into the next 3 sts to the end of the row (these are the opposite sts from the previous 3 rows), tr in top ch of turning ch from the row below, ch 2, turn.

Rows 5 and 6: Repeat row 4.

Rows 1–6 make the basketweave pattern. Continue repeating them until the crocheted fabric is the desired length.

SPECIAL ABBREVIATIONS

Front post treble crochet (fptr)

Yo, place hook around the front of the post of the stitch you are working **2a**, yo and pull up loop, yo, pull through 2 loops, yo, pull through 2 loops **2b**.

Back post treble crochet (bptr)

Yo, place hook around the back of the post of the stitch you are working, yo **2c** and pull up a loop, yo, pull through 2 loops, yo **2d**, pull through 2 loops.

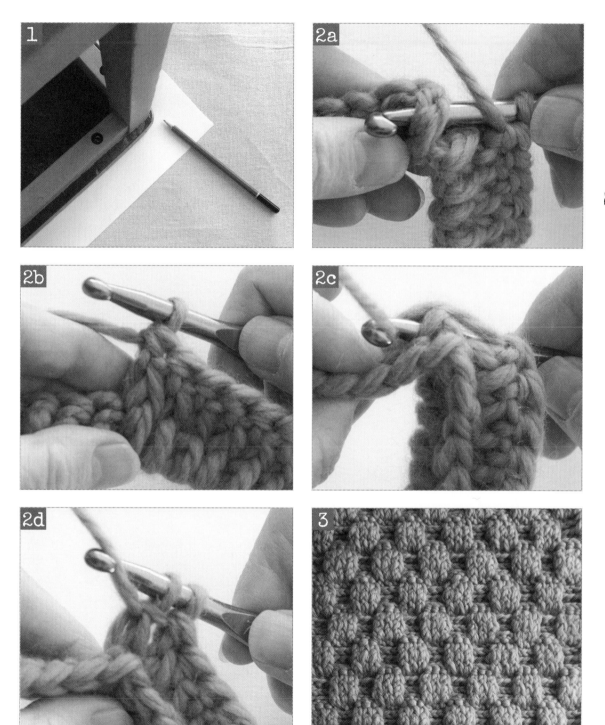

Step 4

Keep the yarn attached and use the 5mm hook to work one row around the edge in dc. If your template is square, make the same number of stitches (a multiple of 3, plus 2 along each edge).

Step 5

On the next 3 rows: *dc along one edge, when you are 2 sts from the corner miss the next st, dc into the corner, miss the next st; repeat from*. Finish off. Finally, use a small crochet hook or a yarn needle to weave in any yarn ends at the back of your work.

OVAL OR CIRCULAR TOPPER

If you aren't confident about adding and subtracting stitches to your work to make it a circular or oval shape, crochet a square or rectangle to fit the largest measurements of the stool top, then cut it to shape and neaten the edges as follows.

Step 6

Start by drawing around the top of the stool on a piece of paper to make a template.

Step 7

Cut out the template and place it on top of your crochet square or rectangle. Use tailor's chalk to draw around the template then use a sewing machine to zigzag stitch the shape of the template on the crochet.

Step 8

Use sharp scissors to trim close to the machine stitching, being careful not to cut into it.

Step 9

Join the yarn again and, using the 5mm hook, crochet a row around the edge using dc. Crochet three more rows, missing out eight stitches evenly around the circumference on each row as you work to reduce the number of stitches. Finish off as before.

See also:

Hand painting *page 132*

Working a foundation chain *page 148*

Double crochet *page 149*

Tension squares *page 150*

Working turning chains *page 150*

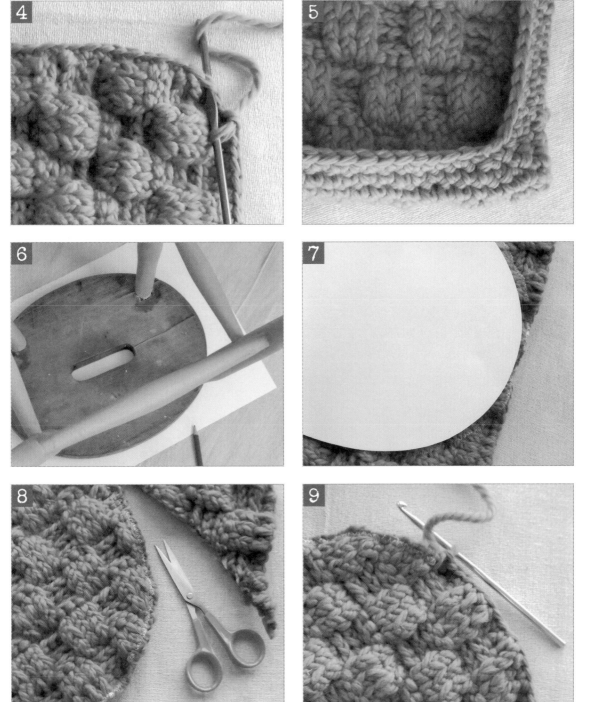

This very easy makeover will completely personalize an old stool by using the photocopied design or wallpaper of your choice. This is a great project for using up favourite scraps and to add an eclectic look to a room.

PAPERED STOOLS

Supplies:
(for a stool top 12in/30cm square)

- ☐ Flat-seated stool
- ☐ Screwdriver
- ☐ WD40
- ☐ Metal paint (such as Hammerite)
- ☐ 1in (2.5cm) paintbrush
- ☐ Fine glass paper
- ☐ Wallpaper samples or colour photocopies of fabric samples
- ☐ Wallpaper paste
- ☐ Soft cotton cloth
- ☐ Lino printing roller (optional)
- ☐ Scalpel or craft knife
- ☐ Matt varnish

TIP

THIS PROJECT WORKS BEST WITH FLAT SEAT SURFACES. YOU COULD ALSO USE THIS TECHNIQUE TO DECORATE DRAWER FRONTS OR A COFFEE TABLETOP.

Step 1

First, dismantle the stool. Hopefully this will just be a matter of undoing several screws. Use a little WD40 to loosen them if they are stiff. If this stage proves difficult, you could carry on without removing the legs.

Step 2

Paint the stool legs with metal paint (standard gloss or eggshell paint will be fine if the legs are wooden). Leave to dry thoroughly, following the manufacturer's instructions.

Step 3

While the stool legs are drying, sand down the wooden top of the stool to make sure it is smooth and free from potential splinters.

Step 4

Cut the wallpaper or the fabric photocopy to measure the same as the stool top plus ⅜in (1cm) all around. Mix up a small amount of wallpaper paste following the manufacturer's instructions. Brush it on to the top of the stool seat.

Step 5

Use a soft, clean cotton cloth to carefully centre and smooth the paper onto the glued surface. Use the cloth to gently push any large lumps of glue or air bubbles to the edge so that you achieve the smoothest possible finish to the paper when it is dry.

Step 6

You could use a lino printing roller to get the surface completely flat. Leave to dry fully.

Step 7

Carefully trim the overhanging paper all the way around the seat with a sharp scalpel or craft knife. Use very fine glass paper to distress the edges and corners of the paper. Prop it up on several egg cups or books before giving the top and sides a few smooth coats of matt varnish, leaving plenty of drying time in between coats.

Step 8

Finally, screw the legs firmly back onto the stool.

See also:

Hand painting *page 132*

Using glass paper *page 128*

Using screwdrivers and screws *page 131*

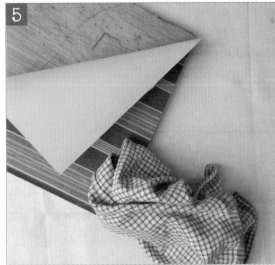

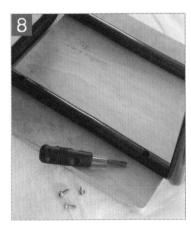

This is a fun and satisfying make. It could provide extra seating at parties and offers useful storage for magazines and books. Old wine crates often feature some lovely branding, notes and numbers to add character.

WINE-CRATE STOOL

Supplies:
(for a standard crate 13¼ x 17 x 9½in/33.5 x 43 x 24cm)

- ☐ 2 x wooden wine bottle crates
- ☐ Pencil, paper and measuring tape to make template
- ☐ Sharp scissors
- ☐ 24in (60cm) of calico (see step 2 for quantities)
- ☐ Sewing thread, needles and pins
- ☐ Iron
- ☐ Stuffing (I used the contents of a hollowfibre pillow)
- ☐ ⅜in (9mm)-thick MDF or plywood (see step 1 for quantity)
- ☐ Fine glass paper
- ☐ Wax paint
- ☐ 1in (2.5cm) paintbrush
- ☐ 4 x small casters or wheels
- ☐ Electric drill and ¹⁄₁₆in (2mm) drill bit
- ☐ Screwdriver
- ☐ Box of ½in (12mm) twin-thread screws
- ☐ 24in (60cm) upholsterer's webbing
- ☐ Crochet yarn: Rowan Pure Linen, 100% linen (142yd/130m per 50g ball); 1 ball in each of shades 391 Kalahari (ivory), 396 Simpson (yellow), 394 Arabian (red), 393 Colorado (green) and 392 Atacama (black)
- ☐ 3.5mm (UK9:US4/E) crochet hook
- ☐ 72in (180cm) of 1⅛in (3cm)-wide woven cotton tape
- ☐ Fabric glue
- ☐ 2 x metal tuck locks or adjustable plastic clips

Step 4

Paint the base, the four edges and a couple of inches around all sides of the top following the manufacturer's instructions. Leave to dry fully.

Step 5

Turn the wood so that it is base side up. Position the casters at each corner, about 1in (2.5cm) in from either edge. Mark the screw holes with a pencil and drill pilot holes with a 1/16in (2mm) drill bit.

Step 6

Use a screwdriver and screws to attach the four casters to the piece of wood.

Step 7

Cut four 6in (15cm) long pieces of upholsterer's webbing (or any similar strong tape). Use two strips to join the crates together. With the crates' bases butting together, screw a piece of webbing 2in (5cm) in from either side and straddling across the join of the two crates' bases. Turn the crates over and repeat the process with two more pieces of tape on the opposite side.

Step 1

Place the two crates on a piece of paper and butt their bases together. Draw around them to make template **A**.

Step 2

To make the cushion pad, cut two pieces of calico the same measurements as template **A** plus 1in (2.5cm) all the way around. Pin or tack the two pieces together and stitch a 3/8in (1cm) seam all the way around, leaving a turning gap of 6in (15cm) along one edge. Turn right side out and press with a hot iron. Stuff with the contents of a pillow. Fold the raw edges around the turning gap in by 3/8in (1cm), tack or pin before closing by hand with overstitch.

Step 3

Use template **A** to mark up and cut out a rectangle of MDF or plywood. Sand all the sharp edges and corners with glass paper.

See also:
Tension squares *page 150*
Changing colour *page 153*
Using screwdrivers and screws *page 131*
Hand painting *page 132*

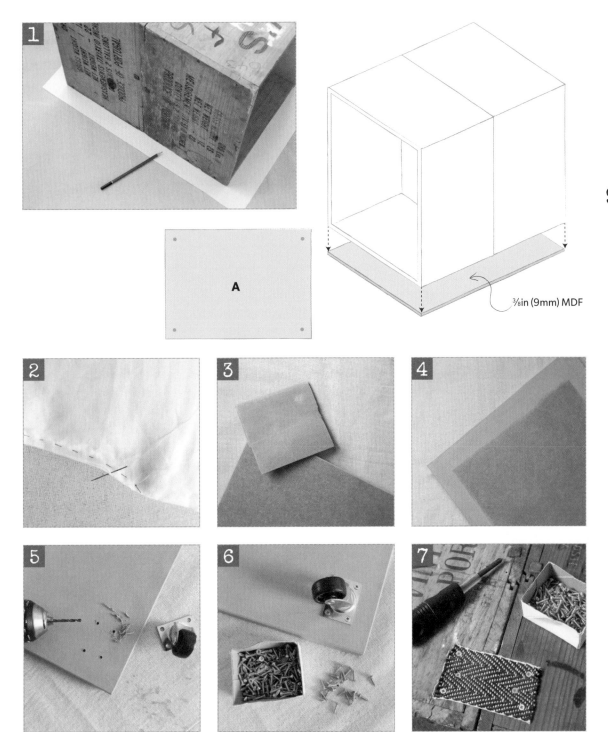

A

⅜in (9mm) MDF

Step 8

Crochet the cushion cover (see Crochet Techniques, page 147). First make a tension square over 15 sts in dc (see page 153). Calculate how many stitches you will need for the foundation chain – this will be the long measurement of your template **A** plus 1½in (4cm) times two. My measurement was 2¾in (7cm), which worked out as 225 ch for my foundation chain.

Make a slip knot and then make the foundation chain. Carefully lay the work down in a circle, making sure there are no twists in it (pinning it out on an ironing board may help) and join into a large ring with a sl st into the first st. You may want to mark this point to recognize it for changing colours for the stripes later.

Step 9

Start working in a spiral, making 1 dc into the top of each st from the previous round.

Step 10

Work 5 rows in the first colour, then change to another colour, changing every five rows at the same point. This creates a slight 'stagger' in the stripes, but this will be lost when positioned at one end of the cushion.

Step 11

When you have completed the crochet to the narrow measurement of template **A** plus 1½in (4cm), keep the yarn attached and flatten out the work with the 'staggered' stripe colour change at one end. Press with a hot iron. Close one of the open sides by using dc and pushing the hook through one stitch from the previous row on the half nearest you, the front, and one from the back.

TIP

TO MAKE A FABRIC COVER, SIMPLY REPEAT STEP 2 USING YOUR CHOICE OF OUTER FABRIC. STUFF IT WITH THE CUSHION PAD THROUGH A TURNING GAP AND AGAIN, CLOSE THE GAP BY HAND WITH OVERSTITCH.

Step 12

When you reach the end, cut the yarn tail to 4in (10cm), pull it through the remaining loop, and use the hook to lose it into the inside of the work.

Step 13

With one edge closed, insert the cushion pad into the crocheted cover through the open edge and then close it up in the same way as done in Step 11.

Step 14

Place the crates on the base with casters, the two openings facing outwards at either end. Place the cushion on top and measure how long to cut the woven cotton tape by wrapping a measuring tape around fairly snugly and adding about 2in (5cm). Cut two pieces of tape to this length with sharp scissors and seal the ends with fabric glue to reduce fraying.

Step 15

Follow the manufacturer's instructions to attach the clips to the ends of the tape before assembling the footstool.

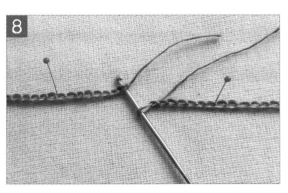

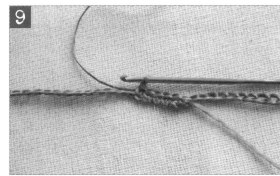

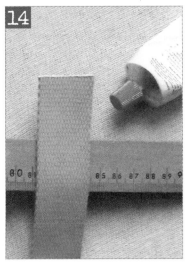

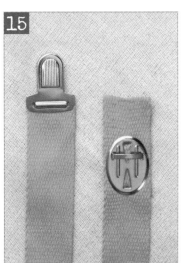

These sturdy seating pads can be used on outdoor seats or simply on the ground. Make yourself comfortable on the porch, early in the morning as the dew lingers, or late in the evening as you unwind.

BOX CUSHIONS

Supplies:
(to make one cushion 17in/43cm square)

- [ ] Scrap of card
- [ ] ⅛in (4mm) hole punch
- [ ] 2 x skeins of embroidery cotton (17½yd/16m)
- [ ] Small crochet hook
- [ ] 60 x 17¾in (150 x 45cm) of deckchair fabric
- [ ] Sharp scissors
- [ ] Sewing needle, sewing thread and pins

- [ ] Sewing machine
- [ ] Iron
- [ ] 8 x 1⅛in (20 x 3cm) scraps of quilt wadding to stuff carrying handles
- [ ] Stuffing (I used the contents of a hollowfibre pillow)
- [ ] Embroidery needle
- [ ] Mattress needle

TIP

STANDARD DECKCHAIR FABRIC IS 17¾IN (45CM) WIDE AND IS REVERSIBLE. THESE CUSHIONS ARE MADE WITH FABRIC THIS WIDTH. YOU COULD USE ANY FABRIC AND ADJUST THE MEASUREMENTS TO MAKE BOX CUSHIONS OF ANY SIZE.

Step 1

First make eight rosettes, following the instructions on page 145.

Cut two 17¾in (45cm) pieces from the fabric to give you two 17¾in (45cm) squares for the top and bottom of the cushion. Now cut four 5½in (14cm) strips – these will measure 18 x 5½in (46 x 14cm) each for the sides of the cushion. Finally, trim the last strip of fabric to measure 17¾ x 2in (45 x 5cm).

Use this last piece of fabric to make the handle. Fold the two narrow ends in to meet at the centre of the strip of fabric and overlap by ⅜in (1cm). Align the raw edges and pin or tack them before stitching ⅜in (1cm) seams. Reverse stitch at the beginning and end of all the seams in this project.

Step 2

Use sharp scissors to snip off the four corners at 45°, taking care not to snip the machine stitching.

Step 3

Use a pencil or crochet hook to help you turn the fabric right side out, gently pushing into the corners to make them sharp.

Step 4

Press the work with a hot iron. Again, using a pencil or crochet hook, push a strip of quilt wadding into the handle through the gap where the two short ends overlap.

Step 5

Use a needle and thread to hand stitch the small gap closed. This is the back of the handle.

Step 6

Use a machine to topstitch around the edge of the handle about 3⁄16in (5mm) in. At the corners, leave the needle down, raise the machine foot and then pivot the work 90° before lowering the foot again and continuing to the next corner.

Step 7

Centre the handle right side up on one of the four 17¾ x 5½in (45 x 14cm) side pieces of fabric, aligning the stripes carefully before pinning or tacking it into position. Topstitch a 1in (2.5cm) square at each end of the handle to attach it securely to the side piece. Stitch each square at least once and make a cross within it by stitching diagonally from the corners.

Step 8

With the handle still facing you, lay another side piece on top and align the two short edges. Pin or tack the two side pieces together along this short edge before sewing a ⅜in (1cm) seam. Start and finish the seam, stitching ⅜in (1cm) from either end, reverse stitching for extra strength.

CUTTING AND ASSEMBLY GUIDE

Top	Bottom	Side	Side	Side	Side	Handle

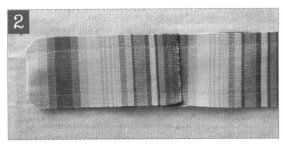

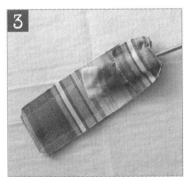

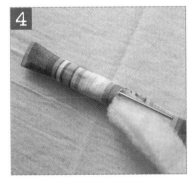

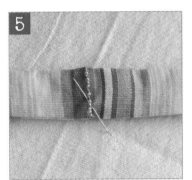

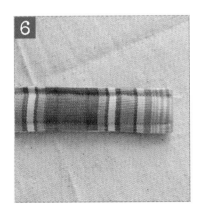

Step 9

Open out the work so the right side is facing you. Repeat Step 8 with the remaining two side pieces to join all four side pieces together in a long strip. Finally, join the two short ends together to create a continuous loop of fabric that will form the sides of the cushion.

Step 10

Lay one of the squares of fabric down in front of you, right side up. Take the loop of fabric from Step 9 and align the long edge of one side along one side of the fabric square. Make sure you put down the right side of the fabric loop. Pin or tack it in position before sewing a ⅜in (1cm) seam along this edge, starting ⅜in (1cm) from the beginning – this will be exactly where the corner seam of the side starts. Sew a ⅜in (1cm) seam along this edge until you reach a point ⅜in (1cm) from the end – this will be where the corner seam of the next side starts. Reverse stitch before removing the work from the machine.

Step 11

Pivot and fold the loop of fabric at the corner of the square so that the next side piece is aligned with the next side. Line up these two long edges, pin or tack them, and sew another seam, reverse stitching at the beginning and end and starting and ending ⅜in (1cm) from either end.

Step 12

Continue in this way around all four sides. Do the same with the other side of the cushion, but this time leave a 10in (25cm) turning gap along one of the edges. Finally, turn the work right side out through the turning gap.

Step 13

Stuff the cushion through the turning gap using the contents of a hollowfibre pillow. Do not overfill, as once you stitch around the edges and attach the rosettes, the cushion will appear much firmer.

Step 14

Fold in the edges around the turning gap by ⅜in (1cm). Pin or tack the gap closed before hand sewing it with overstitch with the thread doubled for extra strength.

Step 15

Thread an embroidery needle with a length of embroidery cotton. Starting at one corner, pinch the seam flat and make fairly large running stitches – about ³⁄₁₆in (5mm) long – through all layers to emphasize the shape of the cushion. Again, this will be more apparent once the rosettes are stitched in place. Do this along all the seams.

Step 16

Mark four points on both the top and bottom of the cushion, 5¼in (13.5cm) in from each corner. Using a mattress needle and a length of embroidery cotton doubled, stitch corresponding pairs of rosettes to both sides of the cushion in the marked positions.

Step 17

Leave an 8in (20cm) unknotted tail of embroidery cotton as you start stitching. Pass the mattress needle back and forth through the cushion and rosettes a couple of times, ending with the needle on the same side you started. Cut off or remove the needle and tug the two thread ends firmly to pull the rosettes snugly into the cushion before tying off and trimming the thread.

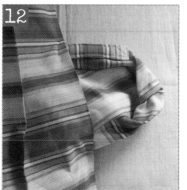

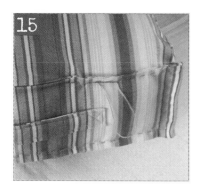

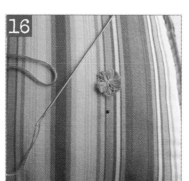

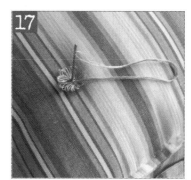

See also:

Basic seams *page 138*
Topstitch *page 137*
Making rosettes *page 145*
Overstitch *page 146*

Transform simple, fold-up chairs with these practical, reversible slipcovers. You could use them for kitchen or dining chairs, too, to add an extra splash of colour for celebrations, parties and special occasions.

GARDEN-CHAIR COVERS

Supplies:
(for a chair back 16 x 16in/40 x 40cm at its widest)

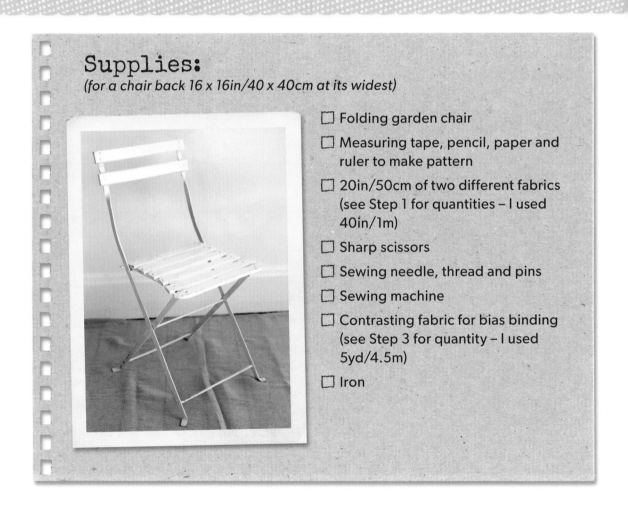

- ☐ Folding garden chair
- ☐ Measuring tape, pencil, paper and ruler to make pattern
- ☐ 20in/50cm of two different fabrics (see Step 1 for quantities – I used 40in/1m)
- ☐ Sharp scissors
- ☐ Sewing needle, thread and pins
- ☐ Sewing machine
- ☐ Contrasting fabric for bias binding (see Step 3 for quantity – I used 5yd/4.5m)
- ☐ Iron

Step 1

To work out your fabric requirements, make your own pattern out of paper (see opposite). Measure the depth of the chair back from its highest point at the back to the bottom of the seat – **A**. Add to this measurement the thickness of the chair back, **B** – probably around 1in (2.5cm) – and the length of the back to the top to where it meets the seat, **C**. Finally, measure the widest part of the chair back – **D**. Draw up a large rectangle on the paper measuring **A** + **B** + **C** + 4in (10cm) by **D**. Cut out the paper rectangle and drape it over the chair back with the extra 4in (10cm) falling below the seat at the back of the chair. Make any adjustments needed to the shape with a pencil, accounting for any tapering in the chair back's shape. Lay the pattern on a flat surface and use a ruler to neaten up the adjustments before cutting away the excess paper. When you are happy with the 'fit', calculate how much fabric you will need.

Using the paper pattern, cut one piece of patterned fabric. Lay the other piece of fabric down and the cut piece on top of it as a template, wrong sides together. Pin them together and cut around them.

Step 2

Tack by hand or run around the edge with a sewing machine to hold the layers in position. Stitch all around the two layers of fabric just ³⁄₁₆in (5mm) or so in from the raw edges.

Step 3

Make the binding – you will need the perimeter of the fabric plus 78in (195cm) in length. Cut 1½in (4cm)-wide bias strips from the contrasting fabric. Cut their ends to 45° angles and join them, right sides together, with ³⁄₈in (1cm) seams, pressing them open with a hot iron.

Step 4

With the bias strip lying right side down, fold it in half along its length – now ¾in (2cm) wide – and press with a hot iron. Open out the fabric again and fold the two long edges in to meet the central crease. Press with a hot iron.

Step 5

Lay the cover over the back of the chair so it falls just below the seat at the back and just touches the seat at the front. Use pins to mark two corresponding positions at each side for the ties, both the back and front. Mine are positioned 6½in (16.5cm) from the top and again 6½in (16.5cm) below that. Make the fabric ties by cutting eight 9in (23cm) pieces of the pressed bias-binding fabric. Topstitch along both long sides of the binding on each piece, encasing the raw edges. Fold one end over twice and stitch down to prevent fraying (this is easier to do with small hand stitches).

Step 6

Pin all eight ties into the positions marked along the raw edges on the side of the work, with the unhemmed short ends aligned with the raw edge of the two layers of fabric and the hemmed tail ends towards the middle of the fabric.

Step 7

Starting just below one corner, tack the folded bias binding around the outside of the fabric. Push the raw edge of the two layers snugly into the fold of the binding as you work. Make a neat mitre at each corner (see page 139). Make sure all the ties are anchored by the line of tacking and extend away from the body of the slip cover. Topstitch through all layers of fabric along the binding, reversing back and forth over the ties to reinforce them.

PATTERN GUIDE

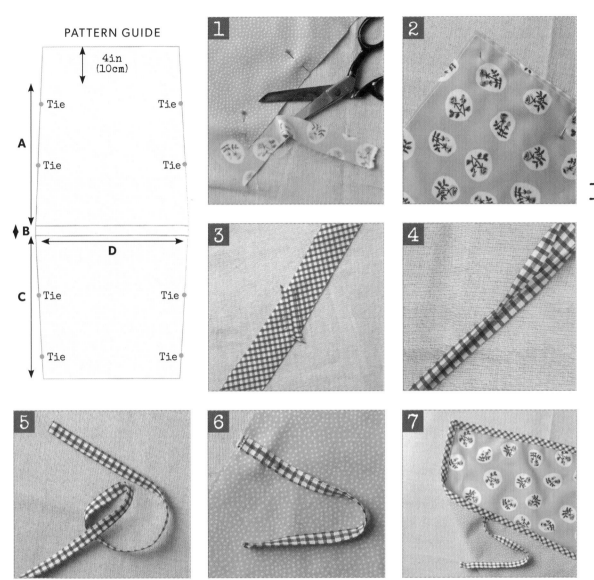

4in
(10cm)

A

B

C

D

Tie   Tie

Tie   Tie

Tie   Tie

Tie   Tie

1

2

3

4

5

6

7

See also:
Making bias binding *page 140*
Making mitred corners *page 139*
Topstitching *page 137*

Give a director's chair a makeover, adding colour and brightness to your porch or yard. The simple Japanese-style sashiko stitching is identical on both sides of the work and the thread ends are hidden neatly in the hems.

110   SASHIKO DIRECTOR'S CHAIR

Supplies:

(for a director's chair with a back measuring 24 x 16¼in/60 x 41cm and a seat 23¼ x 19¼in/59 x 49cm)

- ☐ Folding director's chair
- ☐ Measuring tape
- ☐ Seam ripper
- ☐ Iron
- ☐ 30in (75cm) of upholstery-weight cotton, linen or canvas fabric (see Step 1 for quantity)

- ☐ Sewing needle, thread and pins
- ☐ Sharp scissors
- ☐ Sewing machine
- ☐ 2 x 5⁄16in (8mm) eyelets and fitting kit
- ☐ Pencil and card to make a template for the sashiko embroidery
- ☐ Air-erasable fabric pen
- ☐ About 12 skeins (8¾yd/8m) of variegated cotton embroidery threads to contrast with the fabric
- ☐ Sharp embroidery needle

TIP

YOU COULD MAKE A NEW SET OF FABRIC SLINGS FOR YOUR CHAIR AND EMBROIDER THEM, OR SIMPLY EMBROIDER THE EXISTING ONES.

Step 1

Use the old fabric 'slings' from the director's chair to make a pattern and to work out how much fabric you will need. Unpick all the hems with a seam ripper and press flat with a steam iron. My chair required two rectangles, one measuring 24 x 16¼in (60 x 41cm) for the back, and the other 23¼ x 19¼in (59 x 49cm) for the seat, all including seam allowances. Lay the old slings on the fabric, pin them and cut around them.

With a sewing machine, zigzag stitch (or overlock) around the raw edges of both the pieces of canvas to minimize fraying. This will also help prevent too much bulk when you stitch the hems. Fold over the two long edges of both pieces of fabric ⁵⁄₁₆in (8mm) and then ⁵⁄₁₆in (8mm) again. Press and pin or tack before machine stitching a hem.

Step 2

On both pieces of fabric, fold the two short edges in by 1⅛in (3cm). Press, pin or tack and stitch a seam ¾in (2cm) from the folded edge, and another line of sewing ¼in (6mm) in from this one.

Step 3

Use your old chair slings to mark the position for the ⁵⁄₁₆in (8mm) metal eyelets if your chair requires them. Use the eyelet kit to insert two eyelets, following the instructions on the packaging.

Step 4

Cut a circular template out of card (see below) for the sashiko embroidery and snip out the four notches indicated.

Step 5

Take one piece of canvas and fold it into quarters. Use a hot iron to press the folds. Once opened out, the creases will mark the centre of the fabric. Centre the card template on the pressed creases, aligning the notches on each of the four creases. Draw around it with an air-erasable pen.

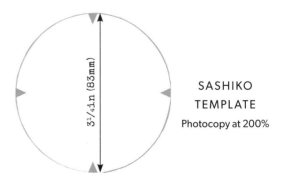

3¼in (83mm)

SASHIKO
TEMPLATE
Photocopy at 200%

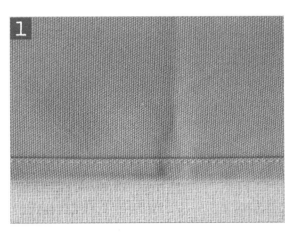

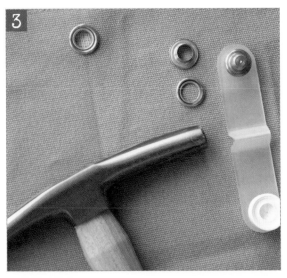

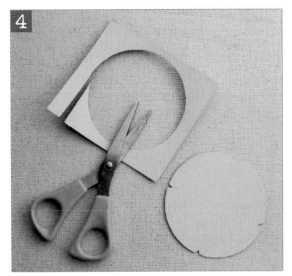

TIP

I DRAW THE END OF AN EMBROIDERY
NEEDLE AROUND THE TEMPLATE TO
'SCAR' THE FABRIC AND USE THIS
INDENT AS A STITCHING GUIDE
RATHER THAN A FABRIC PEN.

Step 6

Draw another circle centred on the vertical crease above, and another below, so that their curved edges just touch each other. Continue in this way until you reach the top and bottom hemmed edges.

Thread an embroidery needle with cotton embroidery thread doubled and knot the ends. The doubled thread should measure about one and three-quarter times the width of the fabric. With the wrong side of the work facing you, push the needle from the stitched edge of the hem through to the folded edge, tugging it firmly so you lose the knot within the hem, the needle emerging at the folded edge at the starting point for the stitching.

Step 7

Turn the work over and use running stitches about ⅛in (3mm) long to follow the drawn lines. Work in a snake pattern, stitching half of each circle at a time.

Step 8

When you reach the far end, turn the work over. Push the needle down through the folded edge, the needle emerging at the back of the work at the top of the hem. Push it back through slightly further along, finally pulling it out along the folded hem edge and trimming it flush with small, sharp scissors.

Step 9

Now work with a fresh length of doubled thread, stitching the other halves of the circles.

Step 10

Continue drawing around the template and stitching, following the interlocking circle design below, until the fabric is covered. The seat is worked in the same way.

Step 11

Give the work a good press with a hot iron before slotting the sticks through the channels along the short edges of both pieces of embroidered fabric. Finally, reassemble the chair.

INTERLOCKING CIRCLE DESIGN

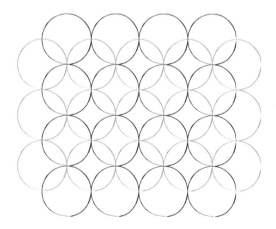

See also:
Zigzag stitch *page 137*
Rivets and eyelets *page 143*

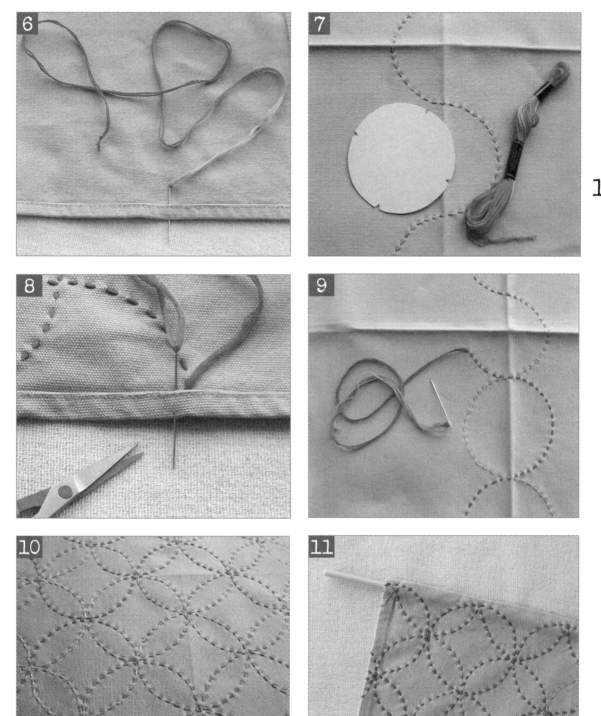

A bright crocheted seat pad will add interest and comfort to a garden bench. Alter the colourway in the crochet squares to reflect the shades in your garden or to add colour when the flowers are fading.

CROCHET BENCH CUSHION

Supplies:
(for a cushion measuring 39⅜ x 15¾ x 4in/100 x 40 x 10cm)

- ☐ Garden bench
- ☐ Rowan Cotton Glacé yarn, 100% cotton (126yd/115m per 50g ball): 1 ball in shade 865 Lipstick (pink) (A) (each square uses 2yd/1.8m), 2 balls in shade 832 Persimmon (orange) (B) (each square uses 4yd/3.6m), 2 balls in shade 867 Precious (purple) (C) (each square uses 4yd/3.6m), and 10 balls in shade 864 Greengage (green) (D) (each square uses 20yd/18.25m) (includes extra for joining squares)
- ☐ 3.25mm (UK10:USD/3) crochet hook
- ☐ Yarn or embroidery needle
- ☐ Iron

- ☐ ½yd (50cm) of backing fabric (I used waterproof fabric to make this project extra versatile; see Step 11 for quantities)
- ☐ Sharp scissors
- ☐ Sewing needle, thread and pins
- ☐ Sewing machine and zipper foot
- ☐ 2 x 16in (40cm) zippers (the length for each should be half the length of the bench minus 4in/10cm)
- ☐ Seam ripper
- ☐ 39⅜ x 15¾ x 4in (100 x 40 x 10cm) foam pad (buy this pre-cut to size: length and width of the seat x 4in/10cm depth)
- ☐ 1yd (100cm) of calico (optional)

CROCHET THE GRANNY SQUARES
Step 1
See page 147 for Crochet Techniques. First make the granny squares. This pattern makes 4in (10cm) squares. You can alter the size by making the them larger or smaller at Step 7. I needed 58 squares – 4 x 10 for the top of the cushion pad, 4 for either end, and 10 along the front edge.

Start with yarn A. Ch 5 and join with a sl st to form a ring. Ch 3 to count as the first treble crochet.

Step 2
Work 15 tr sts into the ring. Join with a sl st to the top of the beginning ch 3 (16 sts). Fasten off.

Step 3
Attach yarn B with a sl st to any tr, ch 1, puff st in the same st and in each tr. Join with a sl st to the first puff st (16 sts). Fasten off.

Step 4
Attach yarn C with a sl st in the closing ch 1 of any puff st, ch 2, (puff st, ch 1) between each puff st from the previous round. Join with a sl st to the first puff st (16 sts). Fasten off.

Step 5
Turn the 'circles' into 'squares'. To crochet a straight line: attach yarn D with a sl st to any ch 1 sp, ch 4 to count as the first dtr st, make 2 dtr sts in the same space, 3 tr in the next ch 1 sp, 3 htr in the next ch 1 sp and 3 tr in the next ch 1 sp, 3 dtr in the next ch 1 sp. This completes one of the four straight lines of the square.

Step 6
To turn the corner: ch 2, make 3 dtr in the same space as the previous 3 dtr in step 5. *3 tr in the next ch 1 sp, 3 htr in the next ch 1 sp, 3 tr in the next ch 1 sp, (3 dtr, ch 2, 3 dtr) in the next ch 1 sp; repeat from * twice.

To finish the last side: 3 tr in the next ch 1 sp, 3 htr in the next ch 1 sp, 3 tr in the next ch 1 sp, crochet 3 dtr sts in the same space as the beginning dtr sts, ch 2, join with a sl st to the top of the beginning ch 4.

Step 7
Ch 1, dc into each st from the previous round along the edge of the square, ending with the last dc in the first ch of the corner ch 2.

Ch 2, dc into the 2nd st of the corner 2 ch, and into all the sts along the next edge.

Continue in this fashion until all four sides are worked and finish by making a sl st into the first ch 1. Repeat this round until you have reached the desired dimensions for your square. I worked four rounds to attain a square measuring 4 x 4in (10 x 10cm). Repeat Steps 1–7 to make all the squares.

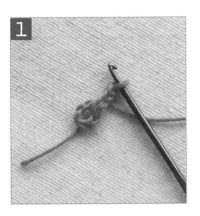

See also:
Inserting a zipper *page 142*
Crochet techniques *page 147*
Overstitch *page 146*

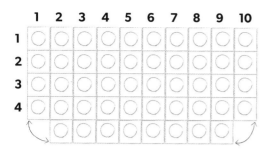

JOIN THE GRANNY SQUARES
Step 8

As with patchwork, it is best to join the squares in strips, and then join the strips together. Lay the squares out on a flat surface. You will have a gap at two of the four corners (see diagram, above). Join yarn D and, working through the top of stitches along the edges of both squares, join the squares together using dc stitches. As you finish joining each square, open out the work and place another square face down on the previous square until all the squares for that strip are joined.

Step 9

Press the work with an iron. Lay out all the strips in position again and work methodically joining the strips together using the method in step 8. Place two strips right sides together, join yarn D and work along one long edge through the stitches of both the front and the back joined strips using dc stitches.

Step 10

Join the corners. On the two corners where a square is missing, fold the work together so that the sides of the two squares either side of the gap align. Join yarn D and, using the same method as before, crochet along this edge to join the two pieces. Fasten off and weave in all yarn ends with a yarn or embroidery needle.

MAKE THE BENCH SEAT
Step 11

Make the back of the bench seat. Cut two pieces of backing fabric (2 x template **B**, see below) 2¾in (7cm) wide and the length of the foam pad plus ¾in (2cm). Place them together, right sides facing, and pin or tack them along one long edge. Sew a ⅜in (1cm) seam at each end, 4in (10cm) long. Reverse stitch at either end for strength. Now change the machine stitch to the longest setting and stitch a ⅜in (1cm) seam in the gap between the two 4in (10cm) seams – do not reverse stitch, as this is just a temporary seam.

Step 12

With the wrong side up, press the seam open and mark the midpoint along it with a pin. Lay both zippers face down along the pressed seam so that their ends are about ⅜in (1cm) apart at the marked centre point. Tack the zippers down so that their teeth lie over the stitch line of the temporary seam.

FABRIC CUTTING GUIDE
For crochet-top cover, cut: 1 x **A**, 2 x **B**
For all-fabric cover, cut: 2 x **A**, 2 x **B**, 1 x **C** and 2 x **D**

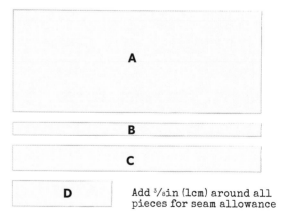

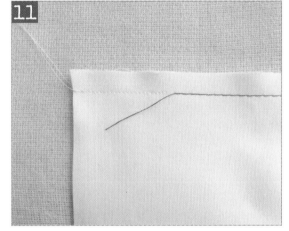

TIP

FOR AN EXTRA-QUICK CUSHION,
MAKE THE WHOLE COVER OUT OF
FABRIC - SIMPLY CUT THE FABRIC
FOLLOWING THE TEMPLATE FOR
AN ALL-FABRIC COVER OPPOSITE.

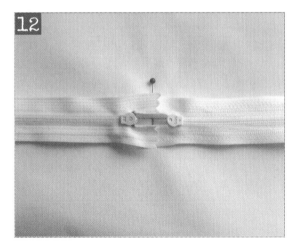

Step 13

Turn the work over and, using a zipper foot on the machine, stitch in the zippers roughly ³⁄₁₆in (5mm) from the join of the temporary seam. Reverse stitch a couple of times at the outer end of each zipper for extra strength – they will be under some stress when you insert or remove the foam cushion pad. Use a seam ripper to remove the temporary seam stitching.

Step 14

Make the bottom of the bench seat. Cut a large piece of fabric the size of the top of the foam cushion pad plus ³⁄₈in (1cm) all the way around (1 x template **A**, see page 120). Lay the prepared zipper panel right sides together along one long edge, aligning them carefully, and pin or tack them together. Sew a ³⁄₈in (1cm) seam along this edge, starting and finishing with reverse stitching ³⁄₈in (1cm) from either end.

ASSEMBLY GUIDES

Crochet-top cover

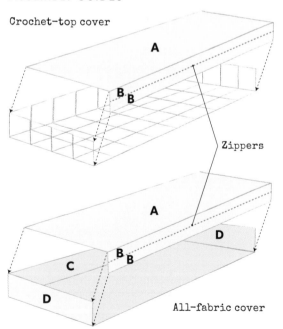

Zippers

All-fabric cover

Step 15

Now join the crochet to the fabric backing. Keep the zippers open a few inches. Place the crochet and the fabric pieces right sides together. Check the assembly guides below to see how they fit together and align all the edges. Pin them at first and then tack them in position ready for stitching. You may find that some squares are slightly stretched (or alternatively need stretching) to fit accurately. The best way to proceed is to mark halfway along the crochet and the fabric with pins and align these points before pinning the two halves together completely.

Step 16

When you reach each corner, pivot and fold the fabrics carefully to ease them around the 90° angles and pin them. You will have two corners where you need to fold the excess fabric and two where you need to fold the excess crochet.

Step 17

Sew a seam all around the pinned or tacked edge. Stitch no more than ³⁄₈in (1cm) from the edge and work from the crochet side to ensure the work doesn't get puckered in the process. Stop the stitching ³⁄₈in (1cm) before each corner, leaving the needle down. Raise the foot and pivot and fold the work underneath until you are in the correct position to continue along the next edge before lowering the foot and stitching a seam along it. Zigzag stitch around all the new edges to reduce fraying of the fabric along the seams. Finally, open up the zippers and turn the work right side out through the opening. Insert the foam pad and close the zippers.

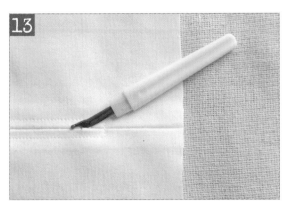

TIP

GIVE YOUR BENCH A FRESH COAT
OR TWO OF PAINT TO SHOW YOUR
PROJECT OFF TO ITS BEST.

TECHNIQUES

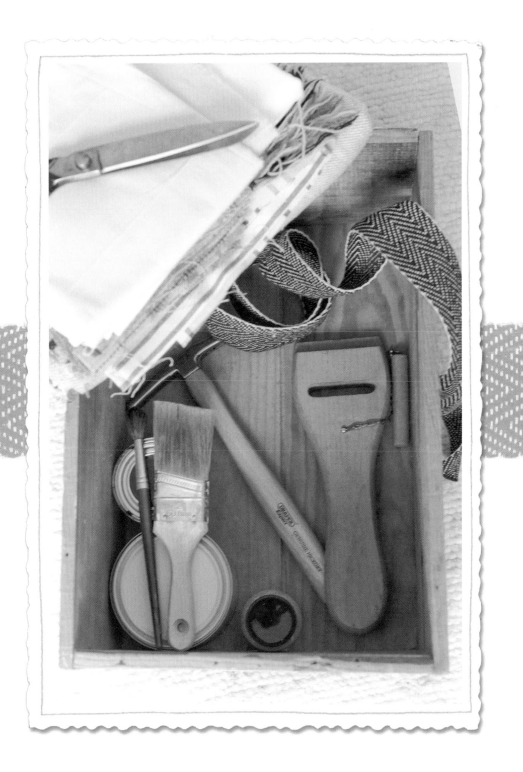

MATERIALS AND EQUIPMENT

You will probably have many of the items you need to make the projects in this book, and anything you don't have should be easily available. As well as the items listed here, a sewing machine will be useful. You will also need a steam iron and an ironing board.

Some of the things you will need include:
yarns (1), trimming ribbons (2), sewing threads (3), staples (4) and staple gun (5), bias binding maker (6), zippers (7), cotton magician's rope (8), crochet hooks (9), screwdriver (10), scalpel (11), strong waxed linen thread (12), self-cover buttons (13), upholsterer's tacks (14), nails (15), twin thread screws (16), tailor's chalk (17), nail puller (18), magnetized upholsterer's hammer (19), mattress needle (20), seam ripper (21), junior hacksaw (22), web stretcher (23), herringbone webbing tape (24) and piping cord (25).

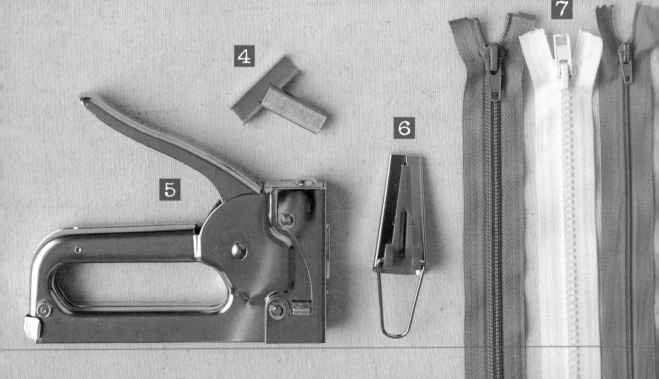

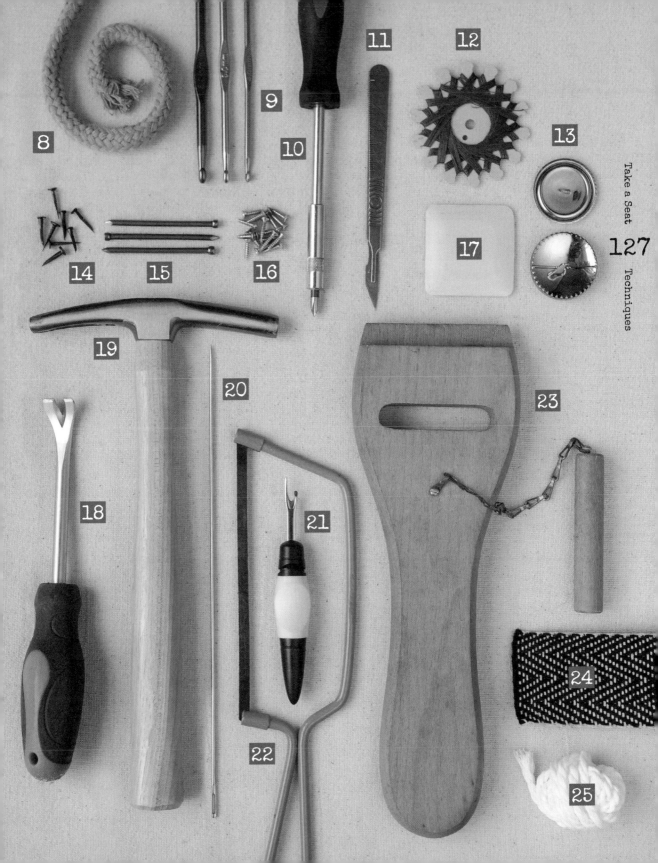

DIY TECHNIQUES

CHOOSING AND RESTORING FURNITURE

There's little more satisfying than bringing a tired old piece of furniture back to life – but always bear health and safety in mind. Check for loose joints; simple nailing and gluing is a quick fix, but more serious wobbles and damage should be looked at by someone with woodworking experience, so do seek help. Try feeling your piece of furniture all over for rough patches. Rub any rough areas or chips back with glass paper (see below). If you are going to paint the piece, fill any dents and cracks with wood filler (**A**), again, rubbing back with glass paper before you paint.

USING A NAIL PULLER

Nail pullers can be really useful for removing tacks and wide-headed nails. Smaller nails, such as panel pins, can be simply hammered flush with the surface.

USING GLASS PAPER

Glass paper (or sandpaper) comes in a range of grades, from very coarse to very fine. It can be used to smooth the surface of wood, filler or paintwork. Start by using a medium or coarse grade paper. Change to a finer grade of paper as the job progresses. Rub the glass paper along the grain of bare timber, not across it, to achieve a really smooth, soft finish.

USING AN ELECTRIC DRILL

Electric drills are very powerful and potentially dangerous. Never wear loose clothing or jewellery that could get caught in the drill while you work. Wear eye goggles to protect yourself from debris. The drill bit will become hot with use, so keep your hands clear of it for a while. Make sure the cable is safely out of the way of the drill bit and unplug the drill before changing to a different-sized bit. Stick a little piece of masking tape over the point you are going to drill to stop the drill from wandering.

Do not drill with one hand while holding the material with the other; ideally, secure your work with a vice. This is not always possible with cylindrical objects, so have someone wearing protective gloves to hold your work firmly. When you drill, apply pressure slowly and steadily to prevent the metal catching and tearing.

USING A SAW

The most important rule of carpentry is: 'measure twice, cut once'. Measure where you want a cut (twice!) and draw a line to act as a guide to help you achieve a straight cut. Don't start the cut directly on the line you marked – cut next to the line on the waste side (the part of the wood you're not going to keep). When you make the first cut, use your thumb or the knuckle of your thumb on the hand holding the wood as a guide to ensure you cut along the cut line (**A**). Draw the saw backwards a few times until you get a nice opening in the wood. Hold on to the handle firmly, but not too tightly.

After you've started cutting, a few short forward strokes will deepen the cut enough for you to move your left hand away from the blade and hold the wood you're cutting at a distance from the blade to steady it (B). Push the saw with an easy, free-running motion. Use long strokes and the whole cutting edge of the saw so that each tooth does a share of the work. Resist the temptation to push down on the saw as it will only tire you out; let the saw do the cutting.

TIP

IT'S BETTER TO CUT YOUR WOOD TOO LONG THAN TOO SHORT – YOU CAN ALWAYS SAND THE WOOD DOWN TO THE PENCIL LINE.

USING AN UPHOLSTERY HAMMER

An upholstery hammer (or tack hammer) is a light hammer used to fix fabric to furniture frames using tacks or small nails. One end of the hammer's head is magnetized to help you position the tacks – this saves holding the tacks in position and risking hitting the ends of your fingers. Tap the nail lightly until the nail has sunk into the wood enough that it can stand on its own. Once started, you can use the other end to finish hammering the tacks flush.

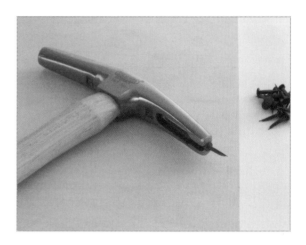

USING WEB STRETCHERS

These are used to make webbing taut across furniture frames for tacking or stapling. Make sure that you feed the webbing through correctly. Place the web stretcher down with the handle to the right and the notch along the left edge facing upwards. Lay the webbing along the stretcher and push a small loop through the vertical slot (A). Turn the stretcher over and hold the loop of webbing in position with the wooden peg (B). You can now use the stretcher to stretch the webbing taut. The tail of the webbing cushions the frame of the piece of furniture (C).

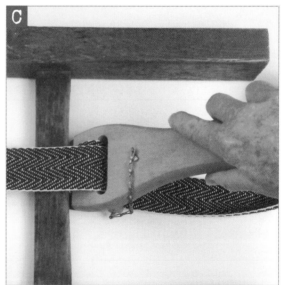

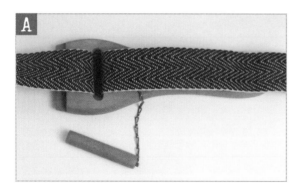

USING SCREWDRIVERS AND SCREWS

Screws can have flat or cross heads (**A**). Always check that your screwdriver head fits really snugly into the slot or cross on your screw head – a loose fit will allow your screwdriver to 'skid' as it turns and risks damaging the top of the screw, making removal or tightening at a later stage difficult. It is useful to get a screwdriver with interchangeable heads like this one (**B**).

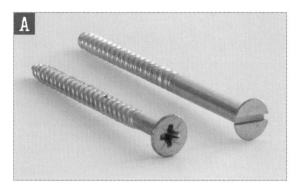

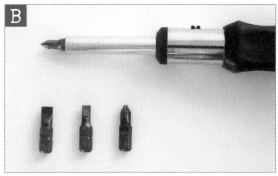

MAKING PILOT HOLES

When using screws it can help to drill a pilot hole first with a fine drill bit; this will prevent the wood from splitting and help the screw 'take', particularly when using hardwoods. The pilot hole should be made with a drill bit of a smaller gauge to your screws to result in a good, tight fit.

Alternatively, you can use a fine panel pin and a hammer to make pilot holes. Take care not to drive them in too deeply with the hammer and keep a pair of pliers or a nail-puller close at hand to help you remove them once the hole is made. Mark your hole positions first in pencil.

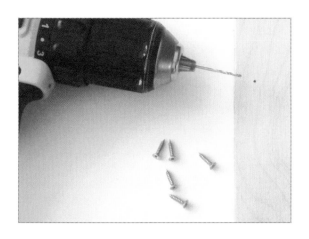

PAINTING

PREPARING SURFACES FOR PAINTING

When you are refurbishing furniture with paint, you will usually need a clean, keyed surface to 'hold' the paint. Keying is achieved by fine sanding and gives the paint something to hold on to.

First give all the surfaces to be painted a wipe over with white spirit or methylated spirit. Then use glass paper to key the surfaces. If the piece is thickly coated with varnish or paint you may need to start with a coarse grade of glass paper (see page 128), then follow up with a finer grade.

If you are using chalk paint, as I have for several projects, the process is a lot easier (see below).

HAND PAINTING

A matt or satin finish is best for furniture, leaving a smart, durable surface. Use a ¼–¾in (5mm–2cm) brush for chair legs and spindles, and up to 1½in (4cm) for larger surfaces. Oil-based paints produce a very strong finish, but cleaning the brushes with white spirit or thinners is a chore – acrylic-based paints make this job much easier.

METAL PAINTS

These paints tend to be oil-based. If you are lucky, you can get away with just one coat – watch out for drips. Be sure to clean your brushes thoroughly with white spirit or brush cleaner.

CHALK PAINT

One coat of this lovely paint is usually enough. It gives a beautiful smooth and solid finish and comes in a large range of colours. It adheres to most surfaces, and there is usually no need to sand or prime before painting, though a wipe down with white spirit or methylated spirit to remove grease is a good idea. Shake the paint, then open and stir it well and follow the manufacturer's instructions. You can finish the chalk-painted surface with soft wax; this deepens the colours, makes the finish more durable and gives it a slight sheen. When you apply the wax, 'push' it into your painted surface with a cotton rag, removing excess wax with a clean cloth. Work small areas at a time, so the wax doesn't dry before you get to work it in. The wax will quickly be dry to touch but takes longer to harden or 'cure'. Follow the manufacturer's instructions carefully.

BUYING AND USING FOAM

A simply shaped piece of foam is fairly inexpensive and can breathe new life into a chair or bench seat but first check out your existing seat pad to see whether it's necessary to buy a new one. If you have a local foam shop, ask for their advice as foam comes in different thicknesses and densities. I used a lovely firm, thick pad on the Coffee-table Footstool (page 76) as it needed to have extra stability. The Crochet Bench Cushion (page 116) can afford to be lighter and thinner for easy storage if you have to tuck it under your arm and run in from the rain!

Get your foam cut to size in the shop, or cut it yourself using a junior hacksaw, a craft knife or a sharp breadknife. There are also some very helpful

and efficient websites you can buy from, taking you through your order step by step and ensuring that you choose the right kind of foam, but be warned – customized shapes can be expensive – it is better to buy a foam pad to your largest dimension and then trim them yourself using a template (see Spoon Seat Pads page 40).

Some suppliers will cover your foam pad with a stocking mesh to give it extra durability and to delay crumbling of the edges with age. It is advisable to give the new foam pad a lining cover, especially if your outer cover is removable. A simple one made in calico doesn't take long to make (see instructions below).

COVERING FOAM PADS

Step 1
Cut a piece of calico the length of your foam pad plus 8in (20cm) and the width x 2 plus 12in (30cm). Fold the fabric in half and align the two long edges. Pin or tack and sew a ⅜in (1cm) seam along this edge.

Step 2
Turn right side out and carefully pull the fabric over the foam pad so that you have equal excess fabric at both ends. Trim the excess fabric to 4¼in (11cm) longer than the foam pad at both ends. Take a little time to fold the ends as you would with gift-wrapping. Make the work nice and snug and pin it firmly in position before using a needle and thread to sew it in overstitch.

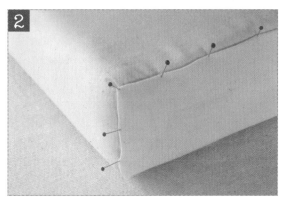

FABRIC

It is incredibly satisfying to use up old fabric such as old curtains and blankets for upcycling projects, but a terrible shame to waste your time and efforts if the fabrics you use are rather past their best. The first, and simplest, test is to hold your fabric up to the sunlight. Look for worn-out patches and moth damage and avoid using these areas of the material – you may still have enough to make a cushion front. You also need to clean the fabric before using it. Natural wools will generally not take kindly to any kind of machine washing, unless your machine has a very gentle hand-wash cycle. Cottons and linens should be washed on a hot cycle and hung out as flat as possible to dry. Press them with a hot iron whilst still damp to get a satisfyingly crisp, flat finish.

HESSIAN
This is a loose-weave fabric used as a base for traditional upholstery.

LINEN
A very strong, supple fabric, this is woven from long flax fibres, which makes it hard-wearing – and it ages beautifully.

WATERPROOF FABRIC
This fabric can be either synthetic or a natural fibre treated with wax or plastics – it is hard-wearing and ideal for garden projects.

WADDING
Used most commonly for quilting, wadding can be made from natural or synthetic fibres. It adds a soft, smooth layer for cushioning.

PRE-SHRINKING
If you are using new fabric and making removable covers (such as for the Graphic Striped Cushions, Sashiko Director's Chair or Crochet Bench Cushion), it is wise to pre-wash it to avoid it shrinking in the wash later.

STAIN PROOFING
Projects with fixed covers (such as the Box Cushions, Coffee-table Footstool or Drop-in Chair Seat) would benefit from stain proofing once completed. This is done very simply with a spray-on stain proofer or retardant. Follow the instructions on the can. Always use stain proofers in a well-ventilated space, preferably outside.

MEASURING

A measuring tape can be substituted with a ruler. Whichever you use, make sure you consistently use either imperial or metric measurements and do not mix the two.

MARKING

You can use an air-erasable pen or a fabric marker. Most fade after a couple of hours, but do check as some need washing out. Tailor's chalk can be brushed away. Use white chalk on dark cloth and coloured chalk on lighter fabrics. The chalk should be kept sharp to produce a clean line. If your design is going to be stitched with a dark thread, you can simply use a very fine, sharp pencil to mark the fabric.

CUTTING

Ideally, you should have two pairs of sewing scissors. A small pair of sharp, pointed scissors is essential for cutting threads and trimming corners and curves. Sewing shears have long blades and a bent handle so that the scissors can rest on the table while cutting, keeping the fabric flat. Make sure your shears are used solely for fabrics and keep them sharp – it is a good idea to get them sharpened every few years.

PINNING

To ensure the fabric will not slip about when stitching, pin and tack seams before you sew, thereby producing a straight, neat seam. Pins with coloured glass heads are easy to find in fabric. Place the pins at right angles to the stitching line if you want to machine stitch over them and avoid having to tack or baste.

TACKING (A)

Also known as basting, this is a temporary stitch used to fix pieces of fabric in position ready for permanent stitching. It is the easiest and quickest hand-sewing stitch. Knot the end of the thread and work large running stitches about ⅜in (1cm) long. Finish with a couple of stitches worked over each other to secure the end. When the seam or hem has been permanently sewn by machine, remove the tacking.

TIP

MARK THE HANDLES OF YOUR FABRIC SHEARS WITH A RIBBON SO THAT NO ONE USES THEM TO CUT PAPER.

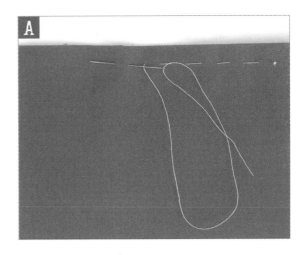

USING A SEWING MACHINE

It is important to keep your sewing machine regularly serviced and covered when not in use. Refer to the instruction booklet for information on threading, changing stitches, reversing, making buttonholes and so on.

A zipper foot is an essential if you don't want to stitch this feature by hand.

Set up your machine somewhere with plenty of light and where you can sit at the machine comfortably.

Before sewing, make sure that the machine is threaded correctly and that the threads from the needle and bobbin are placed away from you towards the back of the machine. Turn the wheel towards you so that the needle is in the work, preventing a tangle of threads as you start. Taking it slowly will ensure control of the machine and make problems with the tension or tangling threads less likely to arise.

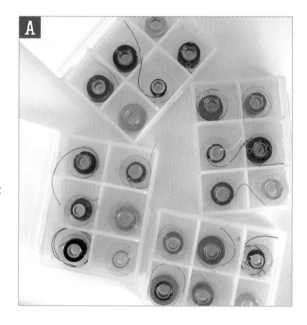

TWO-COLOUR SEWING

I regularly sew with one colour threaded on the machine needle and a different colour in the bobbin below. This is useful when sewing together two different-coloured fabrics, as it makes the stitching less visible on both sides. I keep little pill boxes of fully charged bobbins in all the colours I'll be using in projects (**A**) so I can swap the bobbin over quickly when I need to.

When using this technique it is especially important that your stitch tension is even so that the alternative colours are not pulled through to show on the other side of the fabric.

TIP

IT IS A GOOD IDEA TO KEEP SCRAPS OF THE FABRIC YOU ARE WORKING WITH TO TEST OUT YOUR MACHINE STITCH SIZE AND TENSION BEFORE STARTING ON A PROJECT.

BASIC MACHINE STITCHES

I don't go in for fancy sewing-machine stitching: the basics of straight stitch, topstitch, zigzag stitch and reverse stitch are all you need to make the projects in this book.

STRAIGHT STITCH (A)
Used for all flat seams, hems and topstitching. You can alter the length of straight stitch – at its longest it can be used for gathering or tacking (basting).

TOPSTITCH (B)
This is a line of straight machine stitching worked on the right side of the fabric, parallel to seams and edges. It can be used as both a decorative and a functional stitch, providing extra strength to a hem or seam.

ZIGZAG STITCH (C)
Used along raw edges to help reduce fraying. Zigzag stitches can also be used decoratively or to strengthen points of stress. You can alter the length of the stitches and how close together they are. When changing from straight stitch to zigzag (or vice versa) without breaking your stitching, always adjust your stitch function with the foot down (to hold your fabric in position) and the needle up.

REVERSE STITCH (D)
This reinforces or strengthens the beginning and end of a line of stitching, particularly in areas where pressure or stress will occur. It can also be used as a quick way to start and end stitching without having to finish off thread ends by hand.

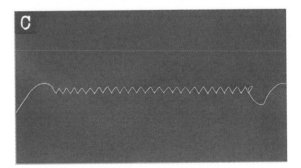

BASIC SEAMS

FLAT SEAMS (A)

Place the two pieces of fabric together, right sides facing. Pin or tack the fabric together. Machine stitch along the sewing line, ⅜in (1cm) from, and parallel to, the raw edges of the fabrics. Finish the beginning and end of the line of stitching either by hand or by reverse stitching.

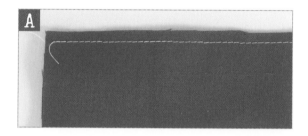

FINISHING OFF THREADS (B)

To finish off ends, thread them onto a sewing needle and either make a couple of small, tight stitches before cutting the thread off, or 'lose' the ends into a French seam or hem.

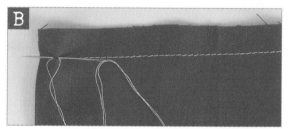

TRIMMING CORNERS AND CURVES (C)

Corners should be trimmed to an angle of 90° so they are sharp when the work is turned right side out. On curved seams, cut V-shapes into the seam close to the stitch line. This will allow the seam to be smooth when the work is turned right side out.

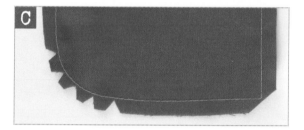

PRESSING SEAMS (D)

Have all the ironing equipment set up before you start sewing. Press each seam as you complete it. Use the point of the iron to open up seams and steam for a crisp edge.

UNPICKING SEAMS (E)

A seam ripper (or stitch unpicker) is a useful tool for unpicking stitches. Several projects require you to use a seam ripper to open the temporary seams in a zipper panel. Insert the pointed blade underneath the thread to be cut. Push it forwards and the blade will cut the thread. It is possible to run the blade along a line of stitching in one movement, but this requires skill and can cause tears.

MAKING MITRED CORNERS

Step 1
Place the two pieces of fabric right sides together. Using a straight stitch, and the indicated seam allowance, sew the side and bottom seams. Pivot at the corners by leaving the needle down, raising the foot and turning the fabric 90°.

Step 2
Press the seams open. With the sewn fabric still right sides together, match the side seam with the bottom fold (or seam) to create a point at the corner. Pin to hold them together. It is very important to match the seams exactly; this will make the finished corner look good.

Step 3
Mark the line of the box corner with a pencil so the depth is measured from side to side at the base of the point. This boxed corner depth is 4in (10cm), measured from the tip of the corner.

Step 4
Sew across the point on the drawn line several times, reverse stitching at the beginning and end for extra strength.

Step 5
Trim away the peak to 3⁄16in (5mm) from the line.

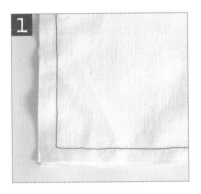

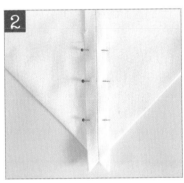

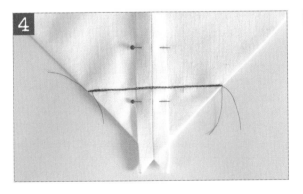

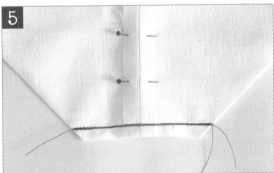

MAKING BIAS BINDING

Bias binding in various widths, colours and patterns is readily available. There are occasions when making your own just adds an extra special something to a project so here is how to make it.

Step 1
Lay your fabric down flat and look carefully at the weave. If you hold the fabric between your two hands and tug it vertically or horizontally (on the grain), it will be firm and have no 'give'. If, however, you pull it on the diagonal, at 45° to the woven threads (on the bias), it will be slightly 'elastic'. Cutting 'on the bias' enables the fabric to curve smoothly on arcs and corners. Cut a square of fabric and draw a line diagonally from one corner at 45° and cut along it. Draw another line parallel to the edge to create a strip the desired width (1½in/4cm in this case) with 45° angles at each end. Draw and cut strips until you have the amount you need.

To join the strips, lay two angled ends right sides together and at 90° to each other. Align the ends and pin them (right sides together if using a patterned fabric). Stitch a ⅜in (1cm) seam to join the two strips. Press the seam open with a hot iron and trim off any excess ends of selvedge to make clean joins in the long strip of fabric.

Step 2
Use a bias binding maker to finish your binding. If you are using cotton lawn or fine cottons, you may want to press the bias strips with starch before using the binding maker. You can make bias binding without the gadget, by folding your long strip in half and giving it a press. Now open it out and fold the two long edges in to meet the centrally ironed crease and press firmly. It is much quicker, however, and more accurate to use the gadget once you have the hang of it.

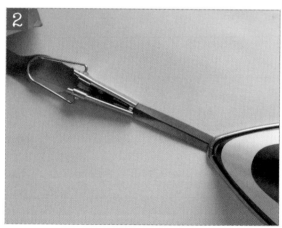

BINDING RAW EDGES

Use tape, bias binding or strips of fabric to bind raw edges. See facing page if you are making your own binding from strips of fabric.

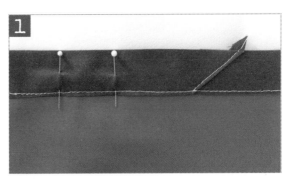

Step 1
Cut the binding to the required length, plus at least ¾in (2cm). Lay it along the edge of your work so that the middle of the binding lies exactly over the raw fabric edge. Pin or tack in position and topstitch ⅛in (3mm) or less from the lower edge. If binding all the way around a piece of work, join it by folding the end under ⅜in (1cm), overlapping the beginning and attaching along this fold.

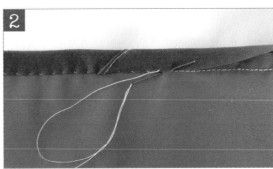

Step 2
Turn your work over. Fold the tape down to meet the stitch line and encase the raw edges. Hem by hand with overstitch.

BINDING AROUND CURVES

Any curved edges require fabric cut on the bias to avoid excessive puckering. The easiest way to do this is to use pre-made bias binding.

Step 1
Open the binding out. Place it on your work right sides together and position the upper fold in the binding along your stitch line. Tack in place and machine slowly and carefully along the fold crease.

Step 2
Fold the binding over the raw edges of your work to the other side. Fold the binding under and hem by hand with overstitch. Press on both sides.

INSERTING A ZIPPER

Step 1

Place your two pieces of fabric right sides together, with the raw edges aligned where you want the zipper positioned. Place the zipper in position along this edge and mark the position of either end of the teeth with a pin. Remove the zipper and pin or tack along the seam, retaining the two marking pins. Stitch a ⅜in (1cm) seam in from either end up to the zipper marking pins, reversing at both these points for extra strength. Now change your machine to a long stitch and sew a ⅜in (1cm) seam between the two markers.

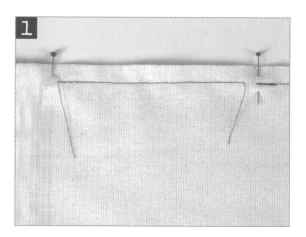

Step 2

Open out the fabric and press the seam open. With the fabric right side down, lay the zipper face down on top centred between the markers. Pin or tack all the way around.

Step 3

Turn the fabric over and sew in the zipper using a zipper foot or a piping foot on your machine. Finally, use a seam ripper to remove the long seam stitches between the two markers.

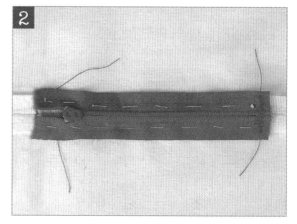

TIP

ZIPPERS WITH METAL TEETH MUST BE THE CORRECT LENGTH – PLASTIC ONES CAN BE TRIMMED TO FIT (AT THE BOTTOM, FIXED END).

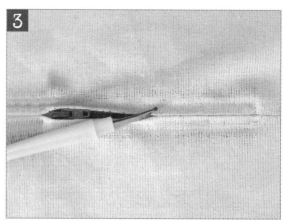

SEWING ON BUTTONS

Mark the position for the button on the fabric. With the thread doubled, tie a knot at the end and pull the needle through to the front of the fabric. Sew the button on securely through the holes, then pull the needle through between the button and the fabric. Wind the thread around the stitches connecting the button to the fabric twice. Insert the needle through to the back of the fabric and finish off with a couple of small, tight stitches.

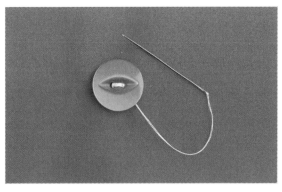

RIVETS AND EYELETS

Metal rivets and eyelets (generally the term used for smaller rivets) can be straightforward to insert into fabric as long as you have all the right equipment. You can buy the rivets in kits and simply need a hammer and a good, solid work surface. First punch a hole in the fabric, then insert the rivet and crimp it to close it firmly around the raw edges of the hole – the punch and crimping forms you need for this come with the packet of rivets (A). Smaller rivets can be applied with rivet pliers bought separately (B). I highly recommend you practise on small scraps of cloth before embarking on your project. Don't scrimp on the type of rivet kit you purchase. The quality of the crimp can make a huge difference.

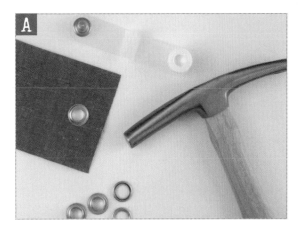

SELF-COVERED BUTTONS

A wonderful way to co-ordinate or contrast buttons is by covering them in fabric. Self-cover buttons have a front and a back piece, plus instructions for the amount of fabric needed for each button.

Step 1
Cut out a circle of fabric at least ⅜in (1cm) larger all the way around than the button front (check the manufacturer's instructions for exact sizing).

Step 2
With the fabric right side down, place the top part of the button centrally on top of it, with the open 'toothed' side facing you. Tuck the edges of the fabric in so that the 'teeth' of the button grip them and the fabric lies smoothly over the smooth surface of the button.

Step 3
Clip the two halves of the button together, using a small pair of pliers if necessary to make sure they are firmly connected.

Step 4
Turn the button over and press and smooth the edges to minimize any wrinkles or tucks.

MAKING ROSETTES

Decorative rosettes are featured in the Box Cushions project (see page 100).

Step 1
Cut a scrap of card to measure 2¾ x 1⅜in (7 x 3.5cm). Punch a ⅛in (4mm) hole ¾in (2cm) in from one short edge, then cut a straight line from the midpoint of the other short edge to the punched hole (see photograph). Feed a 4in (10cm) length of embroidery cotton through the hole – this will be used to bind the rosette.

Step 2
Cut a 75in (190cm) length of embroidery cotton. With the piece of card lying horizontally and the punched hole on the left, wrap the cotton around the narrow width of the card about 25 times.

Step 3
Take the end of the original piece of binding thread that lies at the back of the card and pass it around the right-hand edge, to the front and then to the back again by hooking it through the punched hole with a small crochet hook.

Step 4
Bring the binding thread at the back around the right-hand edge one more time. With both tail ends now at the front, pull them firmly and tie them in a tight knot, snugly against the wrapped thread.

Step 5
Slip the wrapped bundle of threads carefully off the card. Splay out the loops and press out with an iron.

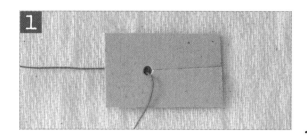

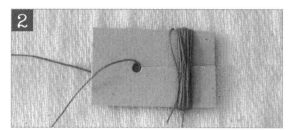

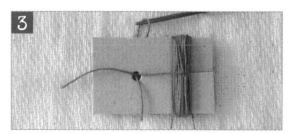

BASIC HAND FINISHING STITCHES

BLANKET STITCH

Step 1
Insert the needle from underneath the selvedge edge on the inside of the work and out at the front through the seam stitching.

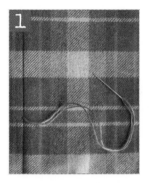
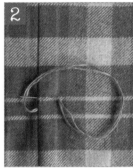

Step 2
Reinsert the needle about ½in (12mm) further along, and ½in (12mm) to the right of the seam. Push the needle out again on the seam line, parallel to where you inserted it, and loop the yarn behind the needle tip. In doing so, check that you have encased the seam selvedge at the back of the work with the yarn.

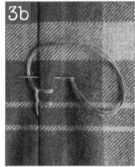

Step 3
Pull the needle through and tug it slightly to create a firm stitch. Repeat.

OVERSTITCH (A)
Use overstitch for closing openings left for turning. With your two pieces of fabric pinned or tacked together, bring the needle up from within one folded edge to the front of the work. Now push the needle diagonally through both folded layers, catching a few threads of fabric from each. Pull the needle and thread through and repeat, spacing your stitches between ¹⁄₈in (3mm) and ¹⁄₄in (5mm) apart.

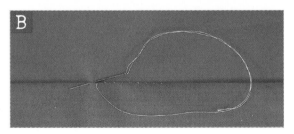

HEM STITCH (B)
Similar to overstitch, this stitch is used for hand-stitching hems.

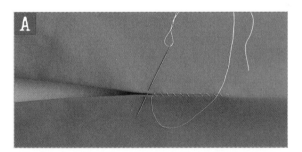

CROCHET TECHNIQUES

HOLDING THE YARN AND HOOK
Keep hold of the work and control the yarn supply with your left hand. Wrap the working bit of yarn under the little finger, over the third finger, under the middle finger and over the index finger. The middle finger feeds the yarn onto the hook (**A**).

When you get into the rhythm of crocheting, you will develop your own way of holding the hook. I hold it in an overhand grip (**B**).

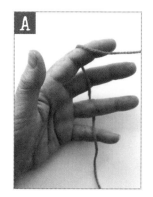

TIP

IF YOU ARE LEFT-HANDED, ALL THE BASIC INSTRUCTIONS GIVEN HERE SHOULD BE FOLLOWED IN REVERSE.

MAKING A SLIP KNOT
A simple slip knot is the starting point for any piece of crochet.

Step 1
Make a loop towards the end of the yarn.

Step 2
Make a second loop and pass it through the first.

Step 3
Pull the top loop to tighten the knot and make it smaller by pulling one of the tails.

WORKING A FOUNDATION CHAIN (CH ST)

Almost all crochet starts with a foundation (or base) chain, a series of stitches like casting on in knitting. From this, you can work in rows or join the chain into a ring to work in the round (see page 155).

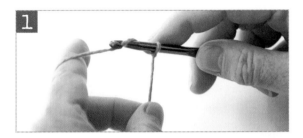

Step 1

Make a slip knot (see page 147), then insert the crochet hook into it and tighten. Hold on to the tail of the yarn with your thumb and middle finger. Wrap the ball end of the yarn clockwise over the hook.

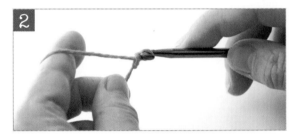

Step 2

Catching the yarn with the hook, draw it towards and through the slip knot to make the first chain.

Step 3

Make further chains in the same way until you have the number required for your pattern. Count the stitches from the front, making sure they are not twisted. Do not count the loop currently on the hook or the initial slip knot.

SLIP STITCH (SL ST)

This is often used to join two pieces of crochet or worked along an edge to prevent it stretching.

Step 1

Insert the hook into the second chain from the hook as shown. Wrap the yarn anti-clockwise over the hook.

Step 2

Pull the yarn through the chain and the loop on the hook in one movement, leaving one loop still on the hook. Work into the next chain in the same way.

WHERE TO INSERT THE HOOK

If you look closely at your crochet chains you will see that each one is made up of two 'strands' forming a V-shape. You can insert the hook under either one (front or back) (A), or both (B) of the strands that make up each individual chain. Unless your pattern states otherwise, pick which suits you best, but be consistent.

DOUBLE CROCHET (DC)

This makes a taller stitch than slip stitch and creates a dense, firm fabric ideal for making items that need to hold a strong shape. Begin with a foundation chain (see page 148).

Step 1

Insert the hook into both strands of the second chain from the hook. Wrap the yarn clockwise over the hook, as for slip stitch (1a). Pull the yarn through the chain (there are now 2 sts on the hook) (1b). Wrap the yarn around the hook again.

Step 2

Now draw the yarn through both loops, leaving one loop on the hook. This completes the first dc stitch.

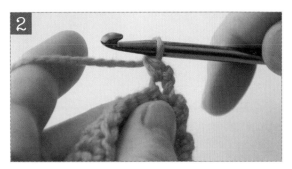

Step 3

Insert the hook into the next stitch and repeat steps 1 and 2 to the end of the row. The hook is now at the left end of your crochet. Before starting the next row, turn the work over so that the hook is on the right again and work a turning chain (see page 150).

TENSION SQUARES

Working a tension square helps to guarantee the size of your finished piece. Make at least 10 chain and work a minimum of 10 rows using the stitch, yarn and hook specified in the pattern. Fasten off and pin out flat, pressing if necessary using a hot iron and a damp cloth. Using a measuring tape, check the number of stitches and rows to 1in (2.5cm). If there are more stitches than specified, try again with a larger hook. If there are fewer, try a smaller hook. If tension is crucial, you may have to substitute thicker or thinner yarn to achieve the correct count.

WORKING TURNING CHAINS

At the beginning of a follow-on row you need to work extra chains to bring the yarn up to the right height for the stitches you are about to work. These extra chains are called 'turning chains'. Without them the row would be too low at one end and your work would become uneven.

The number of chains required depends on the height of the stitch: for double crochet, work one or two turning chains; for treble crochet, which is a taller stitch, work three turning chains.

Step 1

Turn work at the end of a row so that the hook is now on the right with one loop on it. Make a loose turning chain or chains by drawing a loop of yarn through the loop on the hook.

Step 2

For double crochet, work the first stitch of the row into the stitch at the base of the turning chain (2a). For treble crochet, work the first stitch into the fourth stitch of the previous row (2b).

HALF TREBLE CROCHET (HTR)

This forms a stitch height in between double crochet and treble crochet. Work two turning chains at the beginning of follow-on rows.

Step 1
Wrap the yarn around the hook and insert the hook into the top of a stitch from the previous round. Wrap the yarn around the hook.

Step 2
Draw the yarn through (3 sts on hook). Wrap the yarn over the hook again.

Step 3
Draw the yarn through all 3 sts (1 st on hook).

TREBLE CROCHET (TR)

This has a taller stitch than double crochet and creates a more open fabric. Work three turning chains at the beginning of follow-on rows.

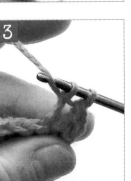

Step 1
Wrap the yarn over the hook and insert it into fourth chain from hook. Wrap the yarn over the hook again.

Step 2
Pull the yarn through the chain (3 sts on hook), then wrap the yarn over the hook again.

Step 3
Pull the yarn through the first two loops only (2 sts on hook) and wrap the yarn over the hook again.

Step 4
Pull the yarn through the last two loops on the hook (1 st remaining on hook).

DOUBLE TREBLE CROCHET (DTR)

This is a tall stitch. Work four turning chains at the beginning of follow-on rows.

Step 1
Wrap the yarn around the hook twice.

Step 2
Insert the hook into the top of a stitch from the previous round. Wrap the yarn around the hook.

Step 3
Draw the yarn through (4 sts on hook).

Step 4
Wrap the yarn over the hook again. Draw the yarn through the first 2 sts on the hook (3 sts on hook).

Step 5
Wrap the yarn over the hook again. Draw the yarn through the next 2 sts (2 sts on hook).

Step 6
Wrap the yarn over the hook again. Draw the yarn through the remaining 2 sts (1 st on hook).

JOINING IN NEW YARN

Drop the old yarn just before working the final 'yarn over' of a stitch, then make the yarn over using the new yarn and pull it through to complete the stitch. Hold down both tail ends until you have worked the next stitch. There is no need to knot them together.

CHANGING COLOUR

Step 1
Drop the previous colour just before working the final yarn over of a stitch, and use the new colour for the final wrap round the hook.

Step 2
Pull the yarn through so the loop on the hook is in the new colour, ready for the next stitch. Continue working in the new colour.

TIP

TO WORK A WHOLE ROW IN A NEW COLOUR, CHANGE YARN AT THE END OF THE LAST STITCH OF THE PREVIOUS ROW TO AVOID CARRYING THE NEW YARN ACROSS THE WORK.

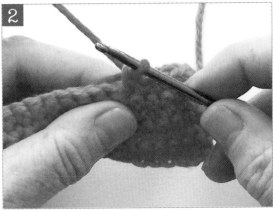

INCREASING (INC)

These are usually made by working two or more stitches into a single stitch of the previous row.

Work the next stitch. Increase 1 st by working into the same stitch again. An extra stitch has now been made.

DECREASING (DEC)

These are made by working two or more stitches together, as follows.

Step 1

Insert the hook into the front thread only of the next two sts, then wrap the yarn around the hook.

Step 2

Pull a loop through (2 sts on hook).

Step 3

Wrap the yarn around the hook again. Pull the yarn through both loops on the hook (1 st remains on the hook).

TIP

INSTRUCTIONS FOR DECREASING IN THE MIDDLE OF A ROW ARE USUALLY GIVEN WITHIN THE PATTERN.

Step 1

Work a foundation chain with the required number of chains (see page 148). Join into a ring by inserting the hook into the first chain, wrapping the yarn over and pulling it through to make a slip stitch.

Step 2

To work the stitches for the first round, insert the hook into the centre of the ring. At the beginning of each subsequent round, make a turning chain (see page 150).

Step 3

From the second round, insert the hook under the top two loops of the stitches in the previous round, unless the pattern states otherwise. Follow the pattern instructions to increase as required. Do not turn your work between rounds.

Step 4

At the end of each round, insert the hook into the top of the starting chain and slip stitch to join into a round again. Work a turning chain (see page 150).

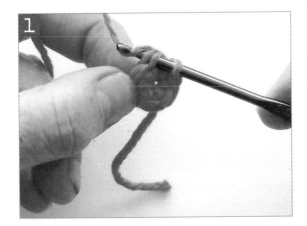

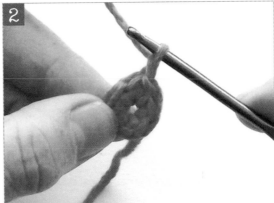

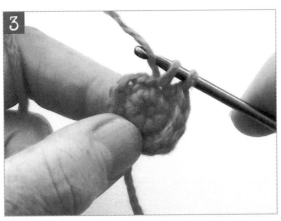

PUFF STITCH

This stitch is featured in the granny squares design of the Crochet Bench Cushion (see page 116).

Step 1
Wrap yarn around the hook and insert the hook into the top of a stitch from the previous round. Wrap the yarn around the hook.

Step 2
Draw the yarn through (3 sts on hook).

Step 3
Wrap the yarn over the hook again, insert the hook into the top of the same st.

Step 4
Wrap the yarn around the hook. Draw through (5 sts on hook).

Step 5
Wrap the yarn around the hook. Draw through (7 sts on hook). Wrap yarn around the hook and draw through all 7 sts.

Step 6
1 st on the hook. Chain 1 to close your puff st (1 st on hook).

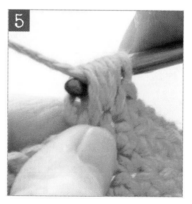

FINISHING OFF

Step 1

Make 1ch and cut the working yarn leaving a 2–4in (5–10cm) tail. Pull the tail through the loop and tighten to prevent unravelling.

Step 2

Use a yarn needle or small crochet hook to weave the tail through the stitches at the back of your work. Cut the tail flush using sharp scissors.

CROCHET ABBREVIATIONS

bptr	back post treble crochet
ch	chain
dc	double crochet
dtr	double treble
fptr	front post treble crochet
htr	half treble
puff st	puff stitch
sl st	slip stitch
tr	treble crochet
yo	yarn over

CROCHET HOOK SIZES

UK	Metric	US
11	3mm	–
10	3.25mm	D/3
9	3.5mm	E/4
8	4mm	G/6
7	4.5mm	7
6	5mm	H/8
4	6mm	J/10
0	8mm	L/11

CROCHET TERMS

UK		US	
dc	double crochet	**sc**	single crochet
htr	half treble crochet	**hdc**	half double crochet
tr	treble	**dc**	double crochet
dtr	double treble	**tr**	treble

Note: this book uses UK crochet terms

Suppliers

YARNS
Rowan Yarns
www.knitrowan.com

ROPE
James Lever Ltd
www.jameslever.co.uk

FABRICS AND HABERDASHERY
Brighton Sewing Centre
www.brightonsewingcentre.co.uk

Endure Fabrics
www.endurefabrics.co.uk

Fabric Rehab
www.fabricrehab.co.uk

Fabric Mills
www.fabricmills.co.uk

Textile Garden
www.textilegarden.com

The Stripes Company
www.thestripescompany.com

The Village Haberdashery
www.thevillagehaberdashery.co.uk

PAINTS AND VARNISHES
Annie Sloan Paints
www.anniesloan.com

Brewers
www.brewers.co.uk

TOOLS AND HARDWARE
Dockerills
www.dockerills.co.uk

Acknowledgements

AUTHOR'S ACKNOWLEDGEMENTS
Thank you to Jonathan, Gilda, Virginia, Nicola, Luana and everyone at GMC who helped in the production of this book, and Emma for her beautiful photographs. As ever, the most thanks to those closest to me, my lovely friends and family, especially the dear old dad, thank you all x

PUBLISHERS' ACKNOWLEDGEMENTS
Thanks to Coats Crafts UK, James Lever Ltd, Fabric Mills and The Village Haberdashery for supplying gorgeous samples.

PHOTOGRAPHY CREDITS
Page 8: Shutterstock/Radiokafka

Index

To place an order, or to request
a catalogue, contact:

GMC Publications Ltd, Castle Place,
166 High Street, Lewes, East Sussex,
BN7 1XU, United Kingdom

Tel: +44 (0)1273 488005
www.gmcbooks.com